D0735654

NINE
YEARS
OF
APPARITIONS
Fr. René Laurentin

Nine Years of Apparitions:

Toward the Revelation of the Ten Secrets?

Latest News of Medjugorje
Number 9
September, 1990

by
Fr. René Laurentin

Translated from French by
Juan Gonzalez, Jr., Ph.D.
Texas Southern University
Houston, TX 77004

Edited and Published by
THE RIEHLE FOUNDATION
P.O. Box 7
Milford, Ohio 45150

The publisher recognizes and accepts that the final authority regarding the apparitions at Medjugorje rests with the Holy See of Rome, to whose judgment we willingly submit.

—The Publisher

Published by The Riehle Foundation
For additional copies, write:
The Riehle Foundation
P.O. Box 7
Milford, Ohio 45150

This book originally published as *"9 Annees D'Apparitions,"* September, 1990 by O.E.I.L., Paris, France.

Copyright © 1991 The Riehle Foundation

Library of Congress Catalog Card No.: 91-065667

ISBN: 1-877678-15-5

Photo Credits:
From French Edition: photos #1, 2, 3, 4, 5, 6, 7.
Tim Schutte: photos #10, 12, 13, 14, 17, 20, 25.
Ken Meymann: photos #8, 9, 11, 15, 16, 18, 19, 21, 22, 23, 24, 27.
Larry Galloway: photos #26, 28, 29.
Jane Derrick: photo #32.

All rights reserved. No part of this book may be reproduced or transmitted in any form without the written permission of the publisher. For information, address The Riehle Foundation, P.O. Box 7, Milford, Ohio 45150.

TABLE OF CONTENTS

FOREWORD
TOWARD THE TENTH ANNIVERSARY

Medjugorje continues to be a place of many conversions, spiritual development and Christian initiatives beginning with the essential: God, prayer and—one may add—fasting.

This grace of God was born in the East like a surprising premonitory sign of the great movement which was going to free Christians from the Church of silence. It was going to (gradually) put an end to the nightmare of a watched, repressed, humiliated, and dangerous life. Undoubtedly, it is not by chance that Yugoslavia, a sensible boundary between East and West in the interior of a Marxist zone, was chosen as the place for this sign in June 1981, well ahead of *perestroika*. During those years, how many other apparitions remained the secret of visionaries or small groups which were hunted down by the police! In Hrushiv (Ukraine), where apparitions took place daily for a year after Chernobyl, enormous crowds came, but we do not yet have any interviews of the visionary. A blurred image and uncertainties remain.

Opposition and Constraints

The sociocultural intelligentsia looks at what comes from on high with scorn, except in the Church itself, especially in the countries of the North Atlantic where demythologization, secularism, and modernism often remain the law and the prophets.

These Medjugorje apparitions, some say, rise from a basic faith, fundamental, archaic, enlightened, visionary. These simplistic and repetitive messages do not take into account the social and political makeup of the world which is the new objective of postconciliar Christians.

Once again God pokes fun at the wisdom of the wise as He did from His humble birth in the crib, then again on the cross. He ironically brings back the wise of this world to

the thoughts of God, which are not those of mankind. Medjugorje is a remedy for a sterile intellectuality which polishes
the faith and converts it again into human, without any intellectual pretensions, to transform the Church of the Saints
into a club of experts...or of free talking people. For the
work of God is measured by faith, love, fruits (conversions,
vocations, initiatives) in order to renew the world and change
hearts.

The event at Medjugorje, which has taken place under a
Marxist government in a rustic small town nurtured more
according to vineyards and tobacco (its crops) than universities, has created one of those great spiritual currents which
restore the Church and make it, through the opening to the
Holy Spirit, its spiritual force.

One asks himself about a paradoxical contrast: why do so
many intelligent, ecclesiastical, and well programmed initiatives ingeniously planted, endowed with finances and well established administrations, remain sterile and sad, void of faith;
and why does the place of pilgrimage of Medjugorje, born
in improvised, uncontrollable, repressed conditions, without
means or infrastructures in a parish in the countryside, change
so many hearts?

It is God's secret, one of those surprises of His kindness.
At times the Holy Spirit produces harvests where one does
not expect them. God is surprising. Medjugorje is the grace
of little David, chosen by preference over his prestigious older
brothers. It is also the grace of a heroic and poor pastoral
who assumed from day to day the confusing event and the
obstacles which had accumulated: the bishop and the government (the Church and State) as well as the unchained international intelligentsia, etc.

The shepherds had been good gardeners. They cultivated
the field of the Lord in spite of the bad conditions and the
hail of blows received.

It is thus nine years from the time that the apparitions began.

A bishop said to me: "This long duration is proof that it
is false."

I have responded to this difficulty elsewhere. But the most astonishing factor is that the event, having taken place in these impossible conditions, has been able to last. The apparitions have been prolonged like a viaticum, on the long way of contradictions: ideology and police of Eastern Europe, iconoclasm of the West, a convergence of theoretical materialism of the Marxist class and the practical materialism of capitalism; skepticism and adverse passions.

Two visionaries have ceased seeing the Blessed Mother (except for an annual apparition): Mirjana on December 25, 1982, and Ivanka on May 7, 1985. The other four have apparitions each evening.

Increase

The large increase of the number of pilgrimages is an obvious fact. One has a good homogenous index of it: the number of communions realized through the hosts of which the parish has been rendering an account for five years:

1985	462,800
1986	596,400
1987	857,000
1988	1,019,000
1989	1,100,000 (a little more than at Fatima: 1,050,000)

The increase has been maintained: 89,000 communions in April 1989, and 140,000 in April 1990. And one has reasons to believe that the cap of 1,000,000 pilgrims a year has been surpassed in spite of the marginal situation of a village far from large highways and railway axis.

Development

This growth and the government's interest in the value of (even winter) tourism is not without its consequences. The unplanned construction gradually disfigured this well known vineyard in its circle of hills. The parish was unable to acquire (as Msgr. Laurence had done), the land necessary to prepare the parish and the future of the place of pilgrimage. Early on, the government "no" to improvements remained invincible and (as Fr. Jozo Zovko complains) the government only gave merchants the authorization to build on what had normally been the open space of the place of pilgrimage.

Business flowed like a tidal wave. Medjugorje did not escape it any better than Lourdes. The children of darkness are more clever and quicker than the children of light. Merchants have often preceded the missionaries and the military in lucrative countries.

The work of the church did not escape the laws of gravity and of the loss of energy. The great spiritual movements often lose vitality by growing and organizing themselves, whether or not the organization is necessary. It is the law of aging: energy decreases while the organization progresses until it is exhausted, empty within its own functioning.

The parish pastoral in Medjugorje struggles valiantly and efficaciously to maintain the essential: purity of prayer, spiritual fervor, and more numerous confessions than anywhere in the world.

Fr. Tomislav Vlasic's pastoral of 1981-1984, founded on God and on the spiritual, became the great period of Medjugorje. He was concerned over it. What should one do so that one's spirit toward God does not become routine? The new communities, inspired by Medjugorje, the countless, always more numerous prayer groups, testify to the fact that this spirit is maintained toward and against everything. The results of nine years of apparitions remain positive.

Since the eigth anniversary celebration (with its record crowds) was covered in our preceding book, let us consider the progress in Medjugorje under its various aspects, according to the plan of the preceding volume: news of the visionaries, inquiries, polemics, spiritual fruits, signs, testimonies, messages, evaluation and the future. The appendices, in which the visionaries themselves will speak, will complete it.

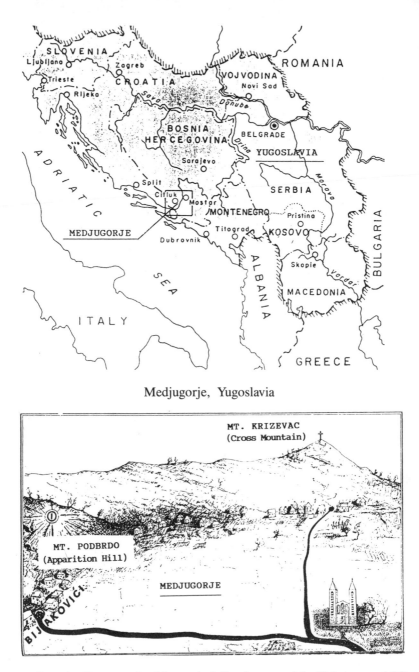

Medjugorje, Yugoslavia

Medjugorje (Between the Mountains) lies between Mt. Krizevac and Mt. Podbrdo, the hill where the first reported apparition of Our Lady took place on June 24, 1981.

Chapter 1

THE NINTH ANNIVERSARY

Since 1986, Ivanka has had a special, annual apparition each June 25 (the anniversary of the first apparition). I had attended each one of the first four. In 1990, as usual, I made the necessary contacts to that effect. I visited Ivanka with Daria Klanac. She was in the process of changing little Josyp, her second child, born 10 days previously on June 14. He is a handsome, blonde, extremely alert baby.

Ivanka was amiable but firm. This year no one would attend the apparition. She had an unpleasant recollection of the intrusion of the previous year. Of course, this crowd was praying, but it literally overwhelmed and the flashes from the picture taking (necessary to leave a souvenir for posterity) had displeased her.

"There will be no one, not even my father," said Ivanka who was persuaded to decide otherwise in the hours which followed.

One could only give in. I asked her only for permission to come in the evening of the twenty-fifth to have news of this fifth annual apparition.

Three Visionaries in the Belfry

This refusal greatly altered my agenda for the day of the twenty-fifth. I had already given up the opportunity to attend the apparitions of the other visionaries. About 5 p.m., I entered the new presbytery (where I had my room) in order to rest before Mass, and as I opened the door, I found myself in front of Ivan and Jakov, who were waiting at the entrance. A Franciscan from the parish came looking for them to prepare for the time of the apparition. He spontaneously asked me what I did not dare ask, knowing that the apparitions arc now without witnesses.

—"Do you want to come?"

I had only to follow and I found myself again in the belfry where I had formerly stayed. I entered the room on the first

1

floor above the choir loft. Msgr. Hnilica, who had arrived from Rome on the preceding night, stayed in this discreet room where the apparition usually takes place.

On this day, a television crew from Zagreb came to make a beautiful reporting of the events. In the tenth decade of the Rosary, which the visionaries recite with the groups, they asked them to come down to the choir loft, which provided more room for their cameras. About 10 minutes to 7:00, all quickly went down on their knees. Their voices, which recited together the *"Our Father,"* faded. It was a lovely dialogue which began for Jakov and Ivan who were elegantly dressed for that feast day. Maria was there also. More silent, more contemplative, she listened to the message which she receives every twenty-fifth of the month, that of the ninth anniversary.

> *Today I want to thank all of you for all your sacrifices and all your prayers. I bless you with my special blessing of a mother. I call on all of you to decide for God, to discover from day to day, His will, in prayer. Dear children, I want to call all of you to a full conversion, so that joy may come into your hearts. I am happy that you are here today in such a great number. Thank you for having responded to my call.*

Mass of the Twenty-fifth

Msgr. Hnilica, a Czech bishop and a man of confidence to the Pope for the selection of bishops from that country (confessors of the faith who now occupy the episcopal seats which were vacant for a long time), had sent his episcopal emblems for the apparition and had laid his pectoral cross and other articles before the visionaries in order to entrust to Our Lady his country and Russia, whose conversion he had at heart. It is he who will preside over the Mass since Fr. Custic is in charge of the announcements and the sermon. Fr. Custic, a Catholic priest from the eastern rite, married, today a grandfather, is the editor of the outstanding Catholic weekly publication, *Glas Koncila*. He speaks forcefully and with a talent that reaches the crowd in its hopes as well as its remorse.

—"I never feared ideological materialism," he said, "for one can respond to its arguments. But today, I fear the practical, more ingratiating materialism."

There was applause. During the offertory, Msgr. Hnilica administered Confirmation to a 48-year-old Puerto Rican, Julio Ruben Ares Torres, who had been baptized the day before in Medjugorje.

The crowd was huge, very dense in the surrounding areas which had been enlarged by the recent purchases and improvements of the parish. In front of me, the setting sun was shining upon the crowd. It will become rose colored as it goes down and disappears during the ceremony. Behind this crowd, the beautiful landscape seems to participate in the gathering of the vineyards, then the woods, and of a line of hills with sweet undulations where there emerges a peak in the shape of a cone with curved sides, which made me think of Japan. These hills slowly turned blue as the sun turned red and faded.

The altar is under the new rotunda where 160 priests are seated (there had been 145 yesterday, June 24). A hundred others heard confessions during the Mass. Confessions had begun, at the beginning of the afternoon, in the new confessionals and on chairs which had been set up here and there in order to meet the demand.

Ivanka's Apparition

Immediately after Mass, which ended at approximately 9:00 p.m., I went to Ivanka's house with Daria Klanac and Dr. Loron, as we had agreed. We left just before the flow of the crowd filled up the streets.

We arrived at Ivanka's outlying home: a new house, the entrance of which is not yet finished (apparent structure of cement). Little Kristina was playing under the entry porch with her dolls. The door remained open. Ivanka's only host motioned us to enter. She was seated on the large sofa in the living room, where I had sat last year during the apparition, almost in front of her. She had changed little Josyp and prepared to give him his bottle. We learned from her the unfolding of this fifth anniversary apparition.

—"It lasted nine minutes. The Blessed Virgin still spoke to me about the fifth secret."

—Why "still"?

—"Last year at this time, she gave me specific details regarding its content. She continued with new specific details."

It is evidently useless to ask which ones. . .Ivanka continued:

—"She did not give me any message for the world, but she blessed the family. Us and our two children. Then she said: *'I thank you for offering your life to create new lives.'* "

The new lives were there: Kristina and little Josyp, right now eagerly engrossed in his bottle for the milk was disappearing.

—"I saw my mother," added Ivanka, very joyful.

(Her mother had died two months before the first apparition.)

—"How long did you see her?"

—"About a minute."

—"Did you embrace her?"

—"No."

—"Touched her?"

—"No."

—"Did she seem happy? Did she smile?"

—"Yes."

Ivanka's beautiful smile eloquently reflected that of her mother.

—"But who attended the apparition?"

—"The four of us with my father and my grandmother."

It is this grandmother whom Ivanka had been living with (until her marriage), and whom the Gospa had asked Ivanka to be good to and to help with the household chores. The Gospa had asked her to do it with all her heart. And in spite of some difficulties of collaboration, she maintained a privileged rapport with her grandmother.

—"And the gentleman, who was at the door, who had us enter, was he present?" I asked.

—"Yes, with his wife," Ivanka answered.

I said to him:

—"How was this privilege bestowed on you?"

—"We received Ivanka at our home in Ireland three years ago, and we came for an extended stay in Medjugorje. She did not want to exclude us."

(His name is Mr. Donnachie, around 50 years of age.)

—"And was Kristina as restless as last year during the apparition?" I asked him.

—"No," answered Mr. Donnachie; "She remained behind her mother, perfectly still."

—"She has learned how to pray," Ivanka stated, "and now when she prays, she is still."

(Ivanka looked at Josyp who was finishing the bottle.)

—"And you, little Josyp, when? I can hardly wait to teach you how to pray."

One of Ivanka's usual hosts, who had not been able to be received this year, had previously told me:

—"The Zagreb television is at Ivanka's; perhaps they want to record the apparition."

—"Did this Zagreb television station videotape the apparition?" I asked.

—"No," answered Ivanka.

—"Did it take any pictures?"

—"No, they had already left by the time of the apparition."

It remains for us to ask some questions with respect to the first apparitions. The most obscure point regards June 30, 1981, which furnished the Bishop his two best objections. On that day, the visionaries believed that the last apparition would take place on July 3. During the questioning of June 30, 1981,

in the evening on her return from the apparition at Cerno, Ivanka was asked who had said that, and she answered:
—"The Gospa" (Our Lady).

"Then this Virgin contradicted herself, so it is not the Blessed Virgin," argued Bishop Zanic.

"How do you interpret the contradiction between this statement and reality—the apparitions have lasted to this day?" I asked her.
—"I do not remember," Ivanka simply said.
—"Then how do you respond to this problem?"
—"I do not know. If I said it, it is undoubtedly that the Blessed Virgin said it. Do not worry about it. God knows. . .We must pray and do everything that we do with love."

The visionaries are strangers to the perspective of history which must laboriously establish the facts and explain them. They are hardly less strangers to apologetics. The Blessed Virgin alone counts for them, and they are indifferent to the factual details of objections or contradictions. Perhaps that is the key to the misunderstandings which exist on this point.

This is not the time and place to dis-entangle the web. A listening of the recording of June 30, 1981 interview shows the condition of the visionaries: exhausted, under pressure, polarized by a knot of inextricable questions without solutions.
—"When will the threats from the police (who were particularly hard the day before) end?"
—"What can one say to this crowd which continues to go to the hill and was frustrated not to find the visionaries there this June 30?"
—"Will it still be necessary to return to this hill where the police forbid going with serious, personal, and family threats?"
—"Will the apparitions be transferred to the Church? This would settle everything."
—And then, "When will they end?" This is the one issue then, conceivable with inextricable problems.

It was in the knowledge of all these concerns that Mirjana said, the morning of June 30, 1981: "Something tells me [that the apparitions will last] three more days. . ."

Such a hypothesis took shape. In the afternoon of June 30, 1981, Mirjana attributed this probability to the apparition, followed by Ivanka who repeated it. The others accepted the idea. Today one cannot drag anything out of the visionaries to better clarify their confusion of the time.

We are far from the inextricable situation of nine years ago, this evening of the ninth anniversary. Ivanka, like the other visionaries (like Vicka who had the apparition at her home), is all joy for this annual visit which has encouraged her to do everything with love. Thus we see her do so with her little Josyp, who grips the finger which I extend to him to tell him goodbye.

Chapter 2

NEWS OF THE VISIONARIES

For the visionaries it is cruising speed. Each one is gradually finding his own personal and spiritual way.

1. MIRJANA

The Wedding

The film cameras were aimed at Mirjana. She was married last September 16, 1989, in Medjugorje.

Why did they conduct such a conspiracy of silence on this long and serious engagement, which had been a public matter for three years? Marco Soldo followed Mirjana like her shadow, a friend and loyal protector. They were shocked or annoyed when I discreetly pointed out this fact. When I talked about it in Medjugorje, it was an obstruction. Was it because Marco, her fiance, was the nephew of Fr. Slavko? And yet there was nothing but honor in this Christian marriage, willfully considered for some time.

In May 1989, at the University of Notre Dame (Indiana, USA), at the time of a large conference on Medjugorje attended by 7,000 people, the Croatian Franciscan priest, Milan Mikulic, unguardedly told me that Mirjana had invited him to bless her marriage on September 16. On my return from America, when I spoke about it at the presbytery of Medjugorje the following month, my interlocutors pretended surprise and skepticism in spite of the evidence which had been previously confirmed to me. The responsibility for information was once again put to the test by announcing the coming event in my book, *"Eight Years."*

It shows how difficult it is (there and elsewhere) to establish serious information when misinformation rises from everywhere, each one wants to substitute what he likes for what actually is.

The marriage of Mirjana Dragicevic, visionary of Medjugorje, to Marco Soldo took place in the parish church of Medjugorje on September 16, 1989. Father Milan Mikulic, OFM, came from Portland, Oregon, to celebrate it. The witnesses were Mr. and Mrs. Gusberti from Switzerland. Three hundred people were invited. According to local custom, every wedding is preceded by a meal offered by the bride at her home, and followed by another meal offered by her husband at his home. Because of the large number of invited guests, the two meals were held at a hunting club near Citluk. The ceremony was celebrated after the reception. Fr. Slavko neutralized the army of photographers during the liturgy. The sermon by Fr. Mikulic began by recalling the history of this marriage.

"As a friend of Mirjana and Marco, back on May 7, 1986, I questioned the six visionaries who were all together here in Medjugorje. I gave them two questions which were written down, to which each of them answered in writing. They had informed me beforehand that Our Lady had left them free to choose their state in life: single, religious life or marriage. Thus she wanted to let them know that all these states of life were agreeable to God. For this reason, I asked them: 'Are you going to serve God in marriage?' Mirjana had answered: 'I do not know.'

"She did not know at that time, but now, three years, four months, and nine days later, she is going to give me her affirmative response by saying: 'I hope to serve God in marriage.'

"She has chosen Marco Soldo as companion for life, to live with him the messages of Our Lady."

Fr. Mikulic adds:

"A nurse from Portland had given me a book on family planning authorized by the Church. When

> I offered it to Mirjana, she said to me: 'I do not
> need it. Marco and I love children, and we will
> have as many as God wants to give us.' "

According to custom, the celebrant presented them with a
Cross, which has its place in every Christian's life. Each one
must be ready to take up that which occurs in this world of sin.

There were many gifts. A friend, who wished to remain
anonymous, gave them a piece of land on which to build a
house, some meters from the place of the first apparition,
on the edge of the village of Bijakovici.

—"It is a special gift from God," said Mirjana.

She had not requested it.

Apparition in America (February 2, 1990)

She and Marco were invited to Portland, Oregon, in the
United States where Fr. Mikulic lives. They had accepted the
invitation to go there in January-February, a slow period for
tourism at the Atlas Agency where she is employed. Fr. Mikulic
wanted her to be there on February 2, because the second
of each month she has an apparition or a locution. It was
not easy because she was pregnant and the United States re-
jects immigration for eventual births which give American
citizenship. The administration blocked the visa.

—"I asked for help from Senator Mark Hatfield. He sent a
fax (teletransmission) to the embassy in Belgrade. . .and I,
my fax to Our Lady."

Mirjana landed in Portland on January 30, 1990. On January 2, the Blessed Virgin had invited her not to have the apparition in the parish church in order to obey the instructions
of Msgr. Zanic on the publicity of the apparitions. With Fr.
Mikulic, she chose then a more private place: the Chapel of
Our Lady of Sinj in the presbytery of St. Brigitte.

Mirjana entered the chapel on February 2, Feast of the
Presentation, genuflected and prayed. Suddenly, her eyes raised

and were fixed on her who came to appear to her. She listened. Her face became sad. Tears fell; then she looked at the objects, medals, and requests placed befor her for Our Lady to bless. She said in a loud voice in Croatian the *Our Father* and *Glory Be*. Then she listened again, nodded her head as a sign of acceptance. Finally, her eyes established contact with the external world. She wiped her tears and left. (The message received is found in Chapter 7.)

The apparition which had begun about 8:10 p.m. lasted from 4 to 5 minutes. (Source: the video cassette of the apparition and the narrative given by the Center for Peace West, Portland, Oregon.) Mirjana left for San Jose, California, on February 5 and returned to Medjugorje a little later.

Apparition in Medjugorje (March 18, 1990)

It was in Medjugorje that Mirjana prepared for the eighth promised apparition on her birthday, March 18. The apparition took place at her home in Bijakovici at 7:15 p.m. It lasted 6 minutes. One could see tears flow several times from Mirjana's eyes. After the apparition she seemed sad: "Why?," I asked.

—"The Gospa spoke to me about the secrets," answered Mirjana, who did not wish to give more details. "She also reminded me of the importance of the Mass; how to live it. She recommended that we pray for unbelievers, those who are far from God and have lost the faith." (Photographic report in *Medjugorje Torino*, no. 32, p. 5.)

Interview of May 30, 1990

I met Mirjana on May 30 in the evening, at her home, with Fr. Petar Ljubicic (the Franciscan whom she has chosen to reveal the secrets) and Dr. Bartulica, a Croatian psychiatrist practicing in the United States. The meeting had been set up, but she had some difficulty receiving us since there was a group of Americans who were staying there and occupied the first floor of her home. After she had arranged it with Marco, she made every effort to find a solution. We went into her large new home in the process of completion, where the living room on the first floor has been halfway completed. There were some chairs and a table around which we were able to sit.

I wanted to try to clarify the error of June 30, 1981: On her return from the apparition at Cerno, she thought that the apparitions were going to end in "three days," on the following Friday, July 4, 1981. It was her personal opinion that morning. "Something told me 'Three days,'" the cassette had recorded.

But that evening, she (and she alone) seemed to attribute it to the Gospa. She did not have a recollection of it and does not present an explanation. It is a matter, it seems to me, of an illusion, explainable by the strained, tiring, traumatizing, exciting conditions of those unexplainable days. Mirjana remembers much less; she remembers that she was at Sarajevo on July 4 (the day on which, it seemed to her, the apparitions would end) and that she had on that day some problems with the police which took up all her attention.

She now has an apparition or locution regularly on the second of each month during her prayers. This meeting often lasts a long time, from two to three hours, usually from 11 o'clock in the evening to 2 o'clock in the morning. Sometimes she listens to the Blessed Virgin speak but does not see her. On April 2, 1990, the Gospa prepared some unknown prayers for unbelievers. She repeated that we are all her children, all equal in her love.

The fatigue in answering the pilgrims' questions weighed on Mirjana, especially now that she is expecting a baby.
—"One has to be amiable, smiling," she said, "but to go somewhere else is a great rest!"

On June 24, 1981, her walk with Ivanka must have taken place about 4 or 5 in the afternoon. They sang on this feast day, but they were worldly songs. They had not carried any transistor or cassettes. When the bishop later asked her to swear on the crucifix to narrate that, she was moved to tears.

I asked her to recall the psychiatric examination by Dr. Dzuda on June 29, 1981, in the hospital at Mostar. On the way to their office, the police showed the morgue to the visionaries. Mirjana recalled her fears before the macabre spectacle:
—"I knew what a hospital was; I was afraid to be locked up by force."

The visionaries herded together into the doctor's office where other people, principally their families, had entered. Dr. Dzuda told Ivanka:
—"You have lost your mother; you had the impression that she was appearing to you!"
—"But I, I did not lose **my** mother, and I saw the apparition," retorted Mirjana.

Like the other visionaries, she did not have the least recollection that Jakov had had a kind of ecstasy during this conversation, as Dr. Dzuda had interpreted it. Zlata, Vicka's mother, who was at the examination with Dr. Dzuda, had received this reproach:
—"What an education you are giving your children! This country of Tito which we have freed in blood, you are going to destroy it!"

Now, Mirjana tells us, "I have seen the doctor again. She gave me the health certificate for the work which I currently do at the tourist agency."

With regard to the end of her daily apparitions (December 25, 1982) and the manifestation of the devil which tried to deceive her one day, she has terrible memories and does not like to speak about it. We also asked her about this kind of parchment, or paperlike material, on which the ten secrets are invisibly written. Would she be able to show it to us?
—"Even if the Commission would request it, I would have to ask the Blessed Virgin first."

She does not have this document here. She left it in Sarajevo in a drawer.

—"I can read it," she said. "But a cousin who had found it at my house believed to have read something there but it was not that."

I am surprised that Mirjana spoke about the secrets again and prepared the mechanism to reveal them (in place since 1984), although, knowing the date, she knew that they would not be revealed very soon.

—"I did it in order to prepare the people for conversion while there is still time, especially for the unbelievers," she responded.

—"But what good is this paper?" I asked.

—"If I die, the revelation will remain."

—"You are young and in good health. That seems to mean that the revelation of the secrets is not very soon?"

At this question, Mirjana smiled and did not answer. Secrets are secrets.

2. IVANKA

Ivanka, who attended her friend's wedding, continues her chores as a mother along with the responsibility for her large house and for the reception of the pilgrims. Her fifth annual apparition took place on June 25, 1990.

From the visits which I made to her on June 24 and 25, I had the impression of great clarity and simplicity. It is that which characterizes her and which grows deep without anything distinguishing her from the other women of this Christian village, except that, more than the others and with a conviction nourished by Our Lady, she does everything, simply, with love.

Her apparition of June 25, 1990, has been narrated in the preceding chapter.

3. JAKOV

The news had circulated (again false news) that Jakov was leaving for military service (through previous commitment) in September 1989 at age 18, and that he had left! It was nothing! I found him again in Medjugorje on Wednesday, May 30, 1990. He had never practiced the trade of locksmith which he had learned at a technical school in Citluk. The parish had found him a job at the bookstore of the pilgrim center; this permitted him to be there for the apparitions.

In March, the Blessed Virgin interrupted her apparitions to Jakov for 10 days, from the twentieth to the twenty-ninth (a day before his departure for Rome). She asked him during these ten days for many prayers for her intentions.
—"Was it hard?" I asked him.
—"Yes. I have never had an interruption previously, except 3 to 5 times at the beginning, for only 1 day."

I told him of Dr. Dzuda's original impression: That he had had an apparition in her office while she was interrogating them on June 29, 1981. Like Mirjana, he was surprised and does not have any recollection of it. On the day after, June 30, 1981, he recalls:
—"When the two young women came to look for us, to take us on a walk, I was scared."

I pleaded that he agree to submit himself to a series of medical studies, provided for in France, which several delays had caused to be cancelled until now. But Jakov has always been negative about it.
—"I have had enough tests for my military service," he objected. And he concluded: "I will pray to the Gospa so that it may not happen."
—I then said, "You will not mind if I pray to her that it may take place if she judges it favorably, for it seems useful to me and for Medjugorje and for the future of discernment on the apparitions."

His departure for military service should have taken place before the end of the year 1990, but he has not been called and does not know anything about it.

4. IVAN

Ivan leads his prayer group which meets Mondays on the Hill of the Apparitions (Podbrdo); Fridays, on Krizevac (that of the Cross), with brief messages and exhortations. They had at one time decided not to disseminate the messages anymore because of their private character, destined for the participants, who hastened to record them and communicate them. This silence could have the advantage of reinforcing the monthly messages from Maria for the world, which finds a large audience among the pilgrims. But the dissemination continues regularly in Italian, in *Eco* and elsewhere. In this documentary book, it has seemed appropriate for us to give at least the most significant messages. It is better to get them discreetly than to allow them to perish.

For a long time, these apparitions on the hill had been the discreet exclusiveness of Ivan's prayer group. They are more and more open to the pilgrims now. At first it was occasional, notably since the annual anniversary of the first apparition. It has now become customary. Crowds in the hundreds, and at times thousands of people, climb these hills each Monday and each Friday with Ivan. Prayer is first of all sung, then there are the first two mysteries of the Rosary (one begins again although the rosary may have already been recited during the parish ceremony). Then there are the *Our Father, Hail Mary, Glory Be to the Father,* during which the apparition (which interrupts them) takes place.

The participants are asked not to take pictures, and the instructions have never been violated. Those who are closest to Ivan recognize the beginning of the apparition because his voice fades then. After the apparition, Ivan confides the message which is immediately translated into Italian, English, German, French. Some write it down. Thus people have made sure that they be effectively disseminated. They bear fruit in hearts which are well disposed through prayer and nocturnal silence.

5. *MARIJA (Maria)*

Maria accompanies Ivan in the prayer group founded by him, of which Maria has been a part since the beginning. She graciously undertook its responsibility during Ivan's military service.

Her life went through a very difficult path in 1988. After she had believed to have enthusiastically found her way in the community of Tomislav Vlasic, near Parma, she left it because of a disagreement. They went in different directions *(Eight Years)*. After an eventful journey in Italy, Spain and France, guided by her friends, she summoned up all her strength in order to have one of her kidneys transplanted to her brother Andrija, who was dying because of kidney failure. This resulted in a new journey: A vain attempt for the surgery to be performed in Italy, and then two trips to the United States, where the operation took place on December 16, 1988. It lasted three hours (accompanied by a long apparition from the Blessed Virgin). Maria had a premonition of this visit of Our Lady who encouraged her plan. She warned the doctor not to be surprised if some anomaly presented itself at his side. But the prolonged apparition was discreet.

This eventful period was for Maria (intelligent and sensitive to all human or spiritual reality) a discovery of the world of which her rustic, poor, and confined childhood had deprived her. So many happenings were met with problems, which the uncertainty of her vocation and future became complicated after the deception with Tomislav. It was a delayed, brief crisis of adolescence, with great outbursts of tonic laughter from the discreet Maria, and joking with her friends.

Post operation fatigue made her stop receiving groups of pilgrims. She began receiving them again at the end of 1989. She accepted these shocks (including the heroic gift of her kidney, which her family and her friends opposed) with a profound wisdom, guided by Our Lady, who does not take away anything of her disposition. Docile Maria, whom Dr. Stopar had chosen (as the most receptive of the visionaries) for a hypnosis without notice, has developed today strong personal and spiritual dimensions and a new personality. She has demanding ideas, even on the spiritual organization of the place of pilgrimage. Her future is promising.

Her friendship with a young Italian, whom she sees frequently, has made it appear to some that she too will follow Ivanka and Mirjana in the path of matrimony. Still a superficial assumption, Maria has well summarized the situation when she says:
—"I am in love only with God alone."

Her friend, with a degree in law, seems to have changed his professional plans and has begun university studies which one does with a view to the seminary. Maria's friendship does not lead through easy paths.

6. VICKA

Vicka, afflicted by a long and mysterious hardship of health which baffled the doctors, was cured of it in 1988, after three years of difficult ordeal (*Eight Years*). The Blessed Virgin had announced to her this cure more than nine months in advance. Vicka had taken the risk of confiding the date in writing to Fr. Bubalo. And it confirmed the mystical character of this ordeal: profound participation in the cross of Christ, without external stigmata.

She took advantage of her recovered health in order to give herself more completely to pilgrims, beyond human limitations. They misunderstand how she values similar discipline with this disposition, this joy, and so many fruits. Of a reactive and impetuous temperament, she happily controls her natural impatience, which daily contacts subject to a difficult test. The patience of her encroached family, which has just built a new house on the edge of one of its fields, is no less surprising.

Vicka is fully committed to the mission which Our Lady gave her. She does not have time to think about her future, and it matters little because Our Lady is guiding her. She is in demand all over the word, but the parish watches over her in order to avoid the separation. As an exception, she was given permission to go and give testimony in Belgium: Banneux and Beauraing on April 7 and 8, 1990, where her influence was efficacious.

7. *JELENA*

I also visited Jelena who has locutions and internal visions "through the heart." It was on May 30, 1990, a little before 8:00 in the morning. She was not fully awakened. This great adolescent, 18 years of age, solid and beautiful, was still tired. She finished her third year in nursing school. Next year she will complete her fourth and final year with the final exam. The prayer group which she founded with Marijana (who had reached the end of her studies as a nurse) consists of 12 to 15 young people, according to the meetings which take place once a month.

—"How is the group progressing?" I asked.

—"It is difficult to say. The main thing is the revelation of the presence of God. One lives it more each day."

—"And the large prayer group" [the one made up of adults in whch she participates]?

—"It meets three times a week: Tuesday, Thursday, Saturday after the evening Mass, for an hour to an hour and a half."

8. *VISITS TO THE FIRST WITNESSES*

Dr. Dzuda, Psychiatrist

On Tuesday, May 29, 1990, I visited Dr. Mulika Dzuda, psychiatrist at the hospital in Mostar, who examined the visionaries on June 29, 1981. She is from a Muslim family as her first name indicates. She is a capable woman. Her office is surrounded by a crowd of patients. But she does not allow herself to be overextended and found the time to receive us at 11 a.m. in the same office where she received (on June 29, 1981) the five visionaries which the authorities had taken to her. . .about the same hour.

—"It was about 10 o'clock in the morning. They were under pressure," she told me.

—"Why did you receive them together? Psychoanalysis of the group?" I asked.

—"I preferred a general conversation. I thought that it was a matter of hallucination and wanted to calm them down, to reason with them together along with some of their parents who were there."

—"Did you conduct any tests? Did you keep a file?"

—"No."

—"During this unique interview, did you reach a conclusion?"

—"Yes, that they were normal. But, with respect to the apparitions, no one in this world can say what they are. It is so easy to transform reality into unreality through fatigue, joy, etc."

—"Have you seen the visionaries again?"

—"No, but I would see them again willingly. It would interest me."

—"They are not far. Did you talk to the bishop?"

—"No. But a journalist from *Ekspres Politika* interviewed me."

The doctor thought that she remembered that Jakov had an ecstasy in her office that morning in 1981.

—"How long did your exam last?" I asked her.

—"An hour."

—"Could you show me where the morgue is which they made the visionaries see before bringing them to you?"

She showed me, to the right of the exit, a single story building, sinister looking at that time. It was renovated in the well kept garden of the hospital. To enter into Dr. Dzuda's office, the visionaries passed in front of the morgue and the police took advantage of it to impress them: a striking argument in order to discourage them from returning to the hill.

Dr. Ante Vujevic

This same May 29, after the visit to Dr. Dzuda, I went to the medical center in Citluk to see Dr. Ante Vujevic, who was the first to examine the visionaries on June 27, 1981. His office was likewise besieged. He led us into an isolated room, opening into a large bay from where one saw Medjugorje. He is a young, nice, prudent man.

—"At that time in 1981, the medical center where we are now, was not built. There was a more rudimentary building. We were on duty three days at a time. I was on duty on the twenty-seventh when the police brought the visionaries. I had heard talk about the apparitions without any particular interest. The village worried about it very much. They asked me for this exam. I did not want to go there. I asked them to bring them to me. A saving of time. They came about 4 p.m. with two police cars plus an ambulance. I spoke with them until 5:30 p.m., a time when they were pressed to leave. I did not hold them. The police were surprised about it. I answered, 'If you do not want them to leave, it is up to you to watch over them.' I spoke with each one of them about a quarter of an hour: first Mirjana, followed by Ivanka. I must have seen also Vicka and Jakov, only five of them, among whom was Ivan. Not Maria."

—"They say that Vicka was in a hurry to leave," I commented.

—"The whole group reacted to leave. Did she insist more than the others? I do not remember."

—"What was the method of your exam?"

—"I asked questions: What did you do? What did you see? Why? according to the information which they submitted to me. I do not have any personal knowledge of the apparitions. My report concluded that these young people were normal, balanced, well situated in time and in space, no hallucinations."

—"Dr. Dzuda thought of a hallucination," the interpreter Sofia observed here. The doctor continued:

—"When I saw them, they were normal. Mirjana, the most tense. The visit to the morgue had impressed her!"

I submitted to Dr. Vujevic the page of my *Account* which recalls his medical exam. He is in agreement with the essentials. I noticed his detailed observations. He does not remember the interrogation of Ivan, perhaps interrupted at the time when he began.

The Priest at the Time of the Apparitions: Zrinko Cuvalo

For the first time, I was able to question Fr. Zrinko Cuvalo who was the assistant pastor (here they say "chaplain") of Fr. Jozo Zovko at the beginning of the apparitions. Since the parish priest was absent, it was he who received the shocking news. This tall Franciscan was hospitable, clear, simple. He spoke extemporaneously.

—"The first news came to me on June 25, about 8 o'clock in the evening. On the twenty-sixth, I had a spiritual retreat in Siroki Brijeg with a group. On my return, I visited the visionaries with three other priests in the home of Mirjana's uncle, opposite Vicka's house. There were many people there. The other priests asked questions but without a tape recorder. I ended the conversation and told the young people to come back. On Saturday the twenty-seventh, about 8 o'clock in the morning, four of them came. Two went to confession. Then I questioned them, this time with a tape recorder; a cassette which I gave to the bishop."

R. Laurentin: I know of it and I used it for my "Account."

Z. Cuvalo: I spoke with them until noon. I questioned them again in the afternoon. Fr. Jozo Zovko returned on Saturday, the twenty-seventh. He listened to the tapes and since then I continued the interrogations with him.

R. Laurentin: What was your opinion?

Z. Cuvalo: I questioned. I told Jozo Zovko: "Open your eyes. . .and the tape recorder."

R. Laurentin: When did you believe?
(A moment of hesitation.)

Z. Cuvalo: The first day, I tried to see what was going on. On Sunday, while I was celebrating a Mass at Surmanski, I said: "The Blessed Virgin is appearing. What is surprising is that she does not appear everywhere. We have become savages although children of God." I began to believe from the very first days. From Sunday, June 28. I had attended the apparition the day before. I had been impressed with the confession of a lady who had come with a blaspheming spirit, since she was unable to understand that Heaven seemed to refuse her a child. Finally, she went to confession. Her confession did not come from her, but from Heaven. They said that I did not believe. Actually, I did not talk about it. I did not want to place any obstacle in the path of God. That only worried me. If I left at the end of a year, it was because of an illness: gallstones, sufferings, overwork. After September 8, 1981, I was questioned by the police from 9 o'clock in the morning until noon. I did not stand up because of my physical problems.

R. Laurentin: Did the bishop believe them?

Z. Cuvalo: In July 1981, he not only believed but he said: "It is clear."

Fr. Umberto Loncar's Diary

I visited Fr. Umberto Loncar at the presbytery in Cerin, St. Steven Parish, with Dr. Bartulica on Monday, May 28, 1990. This Franciscan, close to Medjugorje, has followed the apparitions since June 26, 1981 and has kept a diary in which notations, recorded from day to day, are valuable.

On June 28, 1981, he observed, the crowd was estimated at five or six thousand people on the hill. Some said 10,000. On July 1, the 6:00 p.m. parochial Mass took place for the first time (one was hesitant about this date, but he had noted it the same day). It is on that day that Jakov and Vicka spoke on the microphone at the end of the ceremony. The visionaries said:

—"Do not come in large numbers to the hill. There are some who come and blaspheme."

In fact, on June 28, a man blasphemed, according to a popular rumor, during the apparition. But those who surrounded him reminded him of the dignity of the place and of the event and the blasphemer went down on his knees. Fr. Loncar has heard confessions very often at Medjugorje. He remains deeply impressed with them. He believed very quickly in the apparitions.

On July 2, 1981, the visionaries were questioned severely and threatened with revolvers. On July 3, about 10:30 in the morning, Msgr. Zanic came to Citluk and gathered the priests in order to give them judicious instructions of information and of prudence. At 6:15 in the afternoon, Fr. Loncar went to the presbytery at Medjugorje. He has left us a precise narrative of this apparition, which has been largely ignored and which we give in the appendix.

He noticed the first signs in the heavens which were manifested in Medjugorje, beginning on the third and fourth of August (a testimony which has already been published by Kraljevic, pp. 90-99, to whom I referred in my first book: *Is the Virgin Mary Appearing At Medjugorje?*, in 1984).

The grace of Medjugorje permeates Fr. Loncar and his entire presbytery with peace and with clear faith.

9. THE FRANCISCAN PROVINCE OF MOSTAR

Once again I visited (on May 29, 1990), the provincial house in Mostar. I was informed about the situation of the province which Msgr. Zanic himself described elsewhere in his writings on Medjugorje.

The province has been deprived of its autonomy for years. It cannot elect its provincial according to the democratic constitution of the Franciscan order. The last provincials were named to office (more or less after consultation or a vote which did not have the value of an election), and the provincial does not have the authority of a provincial. He is in some way the delegate of a Franciscan who sits in Rome, in the general house.

It is as if, in one of our villages, the mayor were named by Paris and governed his village dependent upon the authority of an official of the Ministry of the Interior. That is why, after more than 10 years, he who governs the province in Mostar is called Provincial *ad instar,* which can be translated: "like a Provincial."

The last provincial elected according to the rules, Fr. Silic, was dismissed from his charge. He died in exile in Germany. Fr. Pejic, who succeeded him from 1980 to 1988, did his best to reconcile everything. He lived quartered among the irreconcilable. For his successor, a consultation chose Fr. Ferdo Vlasic, who had been imprisoned because of the apparitions. But he was provincial minister only a week and had to resign when he was not approved by the State.

A new consultation chose Fr. Jozo Vasilj, young and generous, a native of Medjugorje, who right away did the impossible in order to grant the bishop what he requested. In a few months, he obtained the resignation of the parish priest of Grude, who maintained himself off and on as head of this parish; the cession of several Franciscan parishes requested by the bishop; the departure of Ivan Prusina who remained in Mostar against the will of the bishop, and had decided to leave only after a judgment had been rendered in good and proper form. But these generous concessions, which remained unilateral, produced anxiety in a certain number of Franciscans and did not appease even the bishop in his struggle. Fr. Jozo Vasilj, overcome by depression, abandoned his impossible functions and left for Zaire, where he teaches in a seminary.

Currently, there is not even a provincial minister in Mostar, but an administration with a vice provincial. That does not facilitate the solution to the problem. As previously, the authorities [powerless for decades] wait and delay so long as the rank and file does its best, not without holding its breath. Is one waiting for a miracle in order to overcome this last obstacle? The last one which it may have?

Chapter 3

INVESTIGATIONS

In the chapter of investigations, it is a stalemate.

A Project In Abeyance

A very beautiful medical and psychological project was underway at the highest level in France, in order to be a paradigm in the study of ecstasies. But it has collided, until now, with the reservation of the visionaries, reinforced by the President of the Commission concerned over the exclusiveness of Croatian doctors.

On their part, the doctors have always shown themselves open and cooperative beginning with the admirable president of the medical subcommittee, Dr. Korljan, invited elsewhere to participate in this scientific experience with those of his colleagues who desired it.

It was useless to insist. Perhaps there still remains a last chance if the promoters know how to take their time to renew relationships at all levels of a complex system: The visionaries, parish, doctors, commission, bishop, Rome. This beautiful project, developed over a long period of time, about which Professor Joyeux had spoken first of all to Cardinal Ratzinger, was called to be the prototype of what would be appropriate to conduct for the medical and psychological examination of the visionaries. The cardinal had understood it well, but remained concerned that it not be a burden on the freedom of Yugoslavs, and especially the visionaries.

The project encountered misfortune after misfortune. In January 1988, the same evening that the visionaries were going to leave for France, plane tickets in their pockets, Maria unexpectedly became ill. Vicka's apparitions stopped for a month. Only one visionary remained—Ivan. This would not have permitted the comparative examinations essential to the project. Since then, the unavailability of some, the opposition of others, the overwork or apathy of another, has postponed the project from day to day: the last time in September 1990. How deceiving and complicated life is! I was sorry that this project remained a lost opportunity, both for Medjugorje and for the study of apparitions.

Of course, for the Blessed Virgin, these scientific studies are a minor thing. During our first stages, she permitted them while leaving the decision to the freedom of the visionaries. Elsewhere, in Italy, in a particular case (which was not a sign of contradiction) she talked them out of it. I think that these studies would be objectively useful, even necessary for decisions and important for the future of reports of the apparitions.

The Official Commission

The commission of inquiry which had been established by the Yugoslav Episcopacy surrounded itself with the greatest discretion. I have said everything that one could say about it in *Eight Years*—Latest News #8. The investigation had substantially ended. There is nothing new since then.

The rumor had circulated that a preliminary decision or publication would appear in March 1990, according to a report from the monthly *Thirty Days* (February). But the month of March passed without having anything new take place. The article from *Thirty Days* allowed first of all a mixed impression. Why did this periodical, open to the supernatural and the apparitions, give a version at least modified on the controversial side of Medjugorje, and importance to objections which have not been clarified?

This article reflected the powerful current of opposition maintained by the action and the statements of Msgr. Zanic who impressed a good part of the episcopal conference and the Roman Curia. In Rome, the opinions were shared. ARPA, the Scientific Medical Association for the study of problems of bioethics, had a large reunion at St. Peter's on the day of the Annunciation, with the presence of two visionaries, Vicka and Jakov. The presence of the Pope was expected. But the office of the Secretary of State objected that, because of the relationship between ARPA and Medjugorje and the presence of the visionaries, the Pope could not commit himself and seem to give a decision on this matter. The misunderstanding would have been particuarly risky because several persons who had spoken with the Pope told of his personal (but unofficial) sympathy for these apparitions (see pages 97-99).

The episcopal commission of inquiry, an improvement over the preceding one, is more free and more open in its labors. Yet the predominance of theologians, more expert in the abstraction and criticism than in the discernment of exceptional facts, allows opinions to be shared, especially since incompletion poses some problems.

At the beginning of March, 1990, Msgr. Zanic, who had reason to fear the recognition of worship in Medjugorje, fruitfully attended by the millions of pilgrims and nearly 100 bishops from throughout the world, published a document in the form of a torpedo against the apparitions. It was a matter of preventing official recognition of the worship. The large Italian weekly, *30 Hours,* had announced that the Yugoslav Episcopal Conference would take a position during its next meeting in March 1990. The question of Medjugorje was actually on the agenda, but no one dared to open a debate which would have gotten nowhere in face of the absolute opposition of the Bishop of Mostar, a man of strong character. Episcopal solidarity made the bishops maintain the status quo. They postponed the decision until later and invited the Commission, once again, to complete its investigation.

In brief, the concern for a good relationship with Msgr. Zanic prolonged the indecision and hardly permitted waiting for an immediate solution (except a new miracle from Our Lady). Msgr. Zanic will reach retirement age on May 20, 1993. One will normally have to wait a little beyond that date in order to work out a solution peacefully.

The positive aspect of this confusing situation is that the place of pilgrimage is prospering and bears fruit in the test. Everyone recognizes its fruits, including Bishop Zanic (who wants to see there only the normal fruits of a good Christian parish). The general opinion of this exemplary worship is equivalent to a recognition by right, since it is well understood that an official recognition of the apparitions has been excluded for the time. It would be difficult to recognize them officially since they have not yet ended, and especially since the great unknown (the secrets) have not been revealed.

Cures

Cures have taken place and have regularly been made known in the parish. To this day there have been some 400. The priests have been overburdened, making it difficult to continue their registration in good order, as had been done for a long time by Fr. Dugandzic, who was promoted to Secretary General of the province of Mostar since 1989.

ARPA (the medical association already mentioned) will take over. It has built an office there in order to establish a Bureau of Records similar to that of Lourdes.

With respect to the official medical commission of the episcopal conference, its president, Dr. Korljan, concerned over its rapid success, is content to select the two most documented files: Damir Coric and Diana Basile (detailed in *Eight Years*). He considers them as constant according to the demanding criteria which govern in the records at Lourdes. In any case, the cures continue.

On the trans-Adriatic ferry which brought me back from Medjugorje on the night of June 26-27, 1990, I met Dr. Antonio Longo, pediatrician, who shared with me his recent cure: a grave fistula which had formed in the intestine (fistula stercoracea enterocutanea). He sent me the file of his cure. This is the substance of his testimony:

> On July 26, 1983, I was operated on as an emergency by Dr. Zannini, for a left hemicolectomy as an ulcer of the colon. The historical examination presented evidence of a grave "dysplasia of the edges" (Prof. Lacobelli). I returned home (after several complications) on October 7, 1983, with the

same fistula; the content of the intestine was escaping into the abdomen. All of that involved great physical and mental suffering while I tried to continue to exercise my medical profession.

A year later on July 26, 1984, I was again urgently hospitalized (resection of the intestine, 90 cm by Prof. Sant Angelo). I returned home on September 20, 1984, again with the open fistula. My family went to Medjugorje to pray for me. [. . .]. I myself prayed, promising Our Lady to go there after my cure. And it is thus that after six years with this open fistula, suddenly from one day to the next, the fistula was closed and stopped seeping the intestinal contents. I was cured. I went immediately to Medjugorje to thank Our Lady. On my return, Prof. Zannini told me, after an examination:

—"You are definitely cured. It is an extraordinary achievement" (narrative of Dr. Antonio Longo, surgical pediatrician, Viale Tiziano, no. 22 80055, Portici, Napoli).

The file contained, particularly, this statement from Prof. J. Bernier: "A stercoraceous fistula, which does not heal spontaneously at the end of six weeks, does not heal again."

Another doctor, Dr. Michele Espinosa from Cibud (Philippines), gives similar testimony of her cure: Having been attacked by cancer which had reached the stage of metastasis, she joined a pilgrimage to Medjugorje in September 1988. Not being able to climb Mt. Krizevac with the group, she decided to wait below. But she suddenly changed her mind:

I said to myself: I am going to go as far as the first station of the cross. If I can go further, I will do it. I was thus walking, to my surprise, from one station to the other without getting very tired. I was overwhelmed by two fears: my own personal fear of dying and the future of my three little children as well as my husband. As I stood before the twelfth station, the death of Jesus, the fear of death disappeared. I was ready to die. I was free. But the fear for my children remained. Before the thirteenth station, where Mary receives in her arms, after his death, this second fear for my children disappeared. Our Lady would take care of them. I was sure of it and I accepted death. I felt lighthearted, at peace, happy like I was before my illness. I came down easily from Krizevac. I returned to the Volli home in order to undergo a medical checkup and the doctors, my colleagues, after an x-ray, told me with amazement:

—"What have you done? There is no longer any sign of illness."
—I burst out in tears with joy and I could only say: "I went on a pilgrimage to Our Lady in Medjugorje."

Two years have passed since then and I feel well; here I am, returning to thank the Queen of Peace (summer 1990).

Luminous Phenomena

The numerous and diverse phenomena and others (specially the "photo miracles"), of which I have gathered a voluminous dossier, are more complex, more difficult to confirm. These phenomena continue, but I can only prudently classify the testimonies while waiting for qualified experts to accept to undertake an interdisciplinary study. These facts have contributed very much to the influence of Medjugorje and have caused a number of conversions. This should not be surprising, seeing the precedent of Fatima.

Chapter 4

POLEMICS

Would the impassioned polemics on Medjugorje be nearing appeasement?

A second volume of a book by Louis Belanger, a polemicist armed with titles in parapsychology, a genius in "public relations," has been announced for three years (see *Eight Years*) but has not seen the light of day at this writing.

Michel de la Trinite

Michel de la Trinite, the thinking brain of the Catholic Counter-Reformation for Fatima, and against Medjugorje, has left the community of Abbot of Nantes in order to enter Grand Chartreuse, according to his first vocation. He has sacrificed his war against Medjugorje for God alone and prayer. May he find in this great religious family the deepest peace. May his prayer also lead the community of the Catholic Counter-Reformation, torn by outrages, back to the Church.

M. Jones and S. N. Rini

Michael Jones (another Michel), author of a virulent book, *The Untold Story of Medjugorje* (*The Hidden Story of Medjugorje*, 2 editions) has not appeared since that time except for rare interviews and purposes which do not add anything to his book. He has allowed his collaborator, Suzzane M. Rini, the responsibility to pursue the polemics in *Fidelity* Magazine (July-August 1990) through a not particularly harsh article in which nothing holds one's attention.

In order to conclude this controversy with his former friend (Michael Jones), who had become his defamer, Dennis Nolan wrote a book. He wrote in it the (recorded) conversations which Jones had manipulated. Jones had sincerely tried fasting on bread and water, which the Blessed Virgin had requested in Medjugorje, but his impetuous temperament did not adapt to it. The influence of the Catholic Counter-Reformation, and Jones' personal taste for polemics and scandal, stirred up the virulence unworthy of this defender of the faith, Dennis Nolan. (*Medjugorje...A Case In Support By Way of Reply,* edition not for general sale, Notre Dame, 1990).

Bishop P. Zanic

Under these conditions, at the beginning of March, I thought I would be able to conclude this short chapter by saying: "At the point in which we are, the polemics have subsided..." And here it was that a particularly vigorous attack came and from a high level. It came again from the Bishop of Mostar, Msgr. Zanic. It was the third (after the *Positio* of April 30, 1984, and the sermon of July 25, 1987). Msgr. Zanic published (at his own expense) 40,000 copies of a pamphlet in Croatian, Italian, English and German (10,000 copies in each language) and distributed it in episcopal conferences and the newspapers of the whole world. Some French friends circulated two different translations, both of them made from the English: one discreetly circulated, the other published totally in tens of thousands of copies in the Catholic Counter-Reformation...deprived henceforth of the tireless Michel de la Trinite.

This severe indictment was entitled: *The Truth About Medjugorje.* We have published this document in the Appendix (cf. p. 179). Msgr. Zanic sent it to the Vatican authorities and orchestrated it with statements and interviews given particularly in Rome on April 29:

—"After the reading of this publication," he stated, "no one and particularly no official, will be able any longer to maintain that these events are supernatural" (*Catholic Herald,* May).

This indictment without concession was light, brilliant, cutting, but edited in the disorder and the excessiveness of a flamboyant passion. Its adversaries could only be liars or blind.

They would be motivated and corrupted by money and sex which reappear in an obsessive manner. This passionate dynamic would deserve an analysis.

The same objections return several times. The denial of cures (3 times) and personal attacks against the visionaries and against those who support Medjugorje: Msgr. Franic, Fathers Jozo Zovko, Tomislav Vlasic (the first two priests responsible for the parish), Fr. Rupcic, Don Amorth, and myself (who would be, with the Archbishop, one of the two columns of this temple of illusions). Msgr. Zanic proceeded impetuously like an archer who is hard pressed, who gathers all his arrows and releases them on his adversaries without taking the time to see if his missiles reached their target. . .or whether they are not boomerangs which destroy those who send them.

For those who would not have the time to read everything, here are the principal topics: The visionaries, the Franciscans, and all the supporters of these apparitions are liars. Their inveterate lies are motivated by money and illustrated with deplorable morals. Medjugorje is comparable to the dangerous sects: In Italy, Mamma Ebbe, recently condemned; and in Guyana that which ended in collective suicide ordered by its guru, Jim Jones. Msgr. Zanic looks for the premonitory signs of this self-destruction. The cures of which they speak do not exist. On the contrary, there are deaths among the sick who have come to Medjugorje. The solar phenomena about which the pilgrims speak are illusory, and they cause the loss of sight to those who look at them. Medjugorje is the fruit of the manipulation of the Franciscans and of the disobedience which flourishes among them.

We do not doubt the sincerity of Msgr. Zanic, trapped by the local internal quarrels in which he became bogged down. We admire his impulse courage and share his ardent concern for the truth.

But one is amazed that this document, published to show the whole truth, hurts the truth in so many ways: Constant misinformation of facts and alleged purposes, a mixture between Medjugorje and deplorable facts in different degrees foreign to the events, inaccuracies and distortions, without speaking of defamations which were badly controlled and which fall, without the author considering it, into calumny. His logic *a priori* supposes and projects the worst on honest laymen and priests who remain astonished over it.

Fr. Jozo Zovko, parish priest of Medjugorje at the time of the first apparitions, was supposedly to have referred to his bishop as a "wolf" and "hypocrite" in the course of the legal proceedings which the communist government conducted against him in 1981 because of the apparitions. But actually, it was the (communist) authorities and not the Bishop at whom Jozo aimed these words. The lawyer for Fr. Jozo has just published a book in defense of his client.

Fr. Tomislav Vlasic (who succeeded Jozo Zovko) was supposed to have called his bishop "Satan." It is true that he is on his guard against Satan, but without advancing similar identification. One wonders how Msgr. Zanic comes to conclude from it when he says, "Satan, it is I who am the target."

One will find in the notes the principal corrections to numerous inaccuracies. I felt repugnance to do this work, but many who correspond with me consulted me about it. It was necessary to do it once and for all, and in good order. I limited the observations to the most salient points.

By way of example, Msgr. Zanic attributed to a Franciscan from Mostar, who had left the order and married a Franciscan nun, the prayer book which is sold in all languages with great success in Medjugorje (a clever way to suggest that the pilgrims were nourishing themselves with the fruit of adultery and sacrilege). But the author of the book is not the ex-priest Ivica Vego, as the Bishop stated; it is exclusively Fr. Slavko Barbaric, a Franciscan of good renown, a great spiritual person, persevering in fasting and prayer. With regard to Ivica Vego's error, it is alas the consequence of seven years of weakening repressions, conducted against this scapegoat. The sanctions obtained against him in 1982, by Msgr. Zanic, forbade him to exercise his priesthood, excluded him from the Franciscan order, and annulled his vows; yes, including chastity. For a long time the priest had protested against this annulment which was decided administratively. He requested a regular judgment, the course of which was annulled by another administrative intervention, foreign to the judiciary and regular canonical process. The sanctions which dispensed him from his vow of chastity under these discouraging conditions finished by being justified in his perseverance.

At the end of such a sad story, would it not be better to afflict oneself and pray for the sinner (who recognized himself as such) than to triumph and to spread this fact before the whole world, while pointing out the name and the place where these religious (reduced to a lay state) would, with difficulty, convert themselves again, in order to raise their family?

The other Franciscan priest, Ivan Prusina, who suffered the same sanctions, obeyed by leaving Mostar at the request of the Provincial—a meritorious sacrifice for he had also strongly decided not to leave the episcopal city of Mostar until a regular judgment had been communicated to him. His sacrifice had hardly been rewarded, for one of the first acts of Msgr. Zanic when he was named administrator of the diocese of Dubrovnik, a neighbor city of Mostar (where Fr. Ivan Prusina had again taken up his priestly functions with the approval of the Provincial), was to communicate to him through the Vicar General, that the three-fold sanction remained. If they had wanted to drive him to the same extreme as his unfortunate friend, what more would one have been able to do? The Provincial who had obtained his placement in Dubrovnik with the hope of reestablishing peace, resigned, seeing the impasse in which he found himself in this matter, as in many others.

These two priests were not from Medjugorje, but from Mostar. It was there that, prior to the apparitions, their differences with the Bishop had risen, prior to the apparitions in Medjugorje.

Reactions and Documents

The reactions to what the majority called the "pamphlet," were numerous and converging.

Msgr. Franic, Archbishop of Split (today retired), who named Msgr. Zanic to the episcopacy in 1970, invited him amicably and paternally to be aware of the errors of theological and moral methods which degraded this well intentioned document.

Daria Klanac, a Croatian exile in Montreal, who had sympathized very much with the powerful and friendly personality of Msgr. Zanic when she went with me to visit him for the first time, expressed to him her astonishment concerning the basis as well as the facts. She had a particularly precise knowledge of them through a study of the cassettes recorded in Medjugorje in the years 1981 and following. Like Msgr. Franic, she defended reputations.

> "Go and see the truth of this place, in Medjugorje! Without fear and without prejudgment. As long as you observe and judge exteriorly, you will not reach a positive solution for the Church and for the world [. . .]"
>
> "From the top of the hierarchy, you have been recommended to observe the events attentively and to keep silence. But you return to such writings. In vain I have searched for the reason, a modest or just judgment, and an objective approach to the problem, for [. . .] there are some recognizable signs [. . .]. Medjugorje is not a hallucination, a lie, an invention, a comedy, a manipulation, a matter of money or of sex. I am sorry to have to write you about it."

The official Catholic journal *Glas Koncila,* always faithful to prudence, expressed surprise in discreet terms:

> "He who will dig up into the private lives of the visionaries and other followers of the shrine, who-

ever scatters to the four winds their weaknesses, real or imaginary, in order to prove by them the falseness of the apparitions, obviously does not observe the method and the practices of the Church, and more particularly, does not fear God Who protects not only against calumny but against defamation. To reveal the sins of others, imaginary or even real, is an evil." (*Glas Koncila,* the Voice of the Council, March 18, 1990, quoted more fully in the appendix.)

Don Amorth, exorcist from the diocese of Rome, became indignant to the point of questioning the mental sanity of the author of the document; he openly demanded his dismissal.

"The priests of the parish who admirably and fruitfully assume the pilgrimage, in spite of the unceasingly renewed contradictions, have written on their part a worthy and respectful letter where they invite the bishop to come and simply see, and cooperate in the work of grace of which they have daily evidence" (text published in the Appendix, p. 215).

In summary:
1. This document, which Msgr. Zanic nobly entitles *"The Truth About Medjugorje"* unfortunately remains silent on the essentil truths: the fact of the apparitions and the graces which flow from them, the positive reports of extensive medical studies on the ecstasy, and on many cures.
2. It devotes itself exclusively to the presentation of the negative side. It casts over Medjugorje many fruits or events foreign to Medjugorje, in a deceptive medley.
3. Its simplifying logic exaggerates, distorts the false number of reported facts.
4. He makes a virtue of spreading evil and invites others to do so.

PSYCHOANALYSIS OF A PASSIONATE DOCUMENT

From the psychological point of view, Msgr. Zanic's polemic (March 1990), struck his readers by its passionate character. A passion is characterized by the opposites which determine it. The polarization of Msgr. Zanic was established, first of all, on the motivations which he attributes to his adversaries: money and sex. He has blurred them in this written document, but he speaks of them more freely in his interviews.

Money

In the pamphlet of March 1990, he explains thus the conduct of the devout in Medjugorje:
—"They have as their goal to collect a lot of money."

In the interview with Kieron Wood for Irish television, he was inexhaustible:
—"I do not have any money to print books [and yet he published 40,000 copies of his latest document and his supporters succeeded in having other translations with a large circulation]. Laurentin and the others are rich, rich, rich liars! All those who have written and published books, filmed and reproduced cassettes, spread the souvenirs, etc., are rich! For money plays a very important role in this matter. Money, money! And the Franciscans have dollars, German marks, lire, francs. . .tremendous" (etc.).

And to Daria Klanac (documented conversation of October 14, 1986):

> *Msgr. Zanic:* They (the Franciscans) have earned money! Piles of money! You know, I hear a little; there are some who tell me. There are piles. They buy propaganda.
>
> *Daria Klanac:* What is the opinion of the Vatican?
>
> *Msgr. Zanic:* I am afraid that Medjugorje is not buying them!

Msgr. Zanic also developed this theme before the French press, which he received in his cathedral, while he stressed that the press had been hiding: a statement which very much surprised (and did not convince) the journalists who were present.

Sex

He accused one of the Franciscans, with Medjugorje in mind, as the father of a child in Germany in spite of the denial by the child's mother.

In a conversation, recorded by Daria Klanac, he accuses a holy priest, Jozo Zovko, of "violating some Italian women in his church." He had imposed sanctions elsewhere against this priest on the basis of accounts without foundation.

In his pamphlet in 1990, he had his most impressive trophy in his trophy case: Ivica Vego, his scapegoat, whose vows he had annulled through administrative sanction. The annulment ended by becoming a reality. This discouraged priest (who had elsewhere recognized his faults) is today married and father of a family. We understand that Msgr. Zanic is triumphantly pleased; but is this something to triumph over?

In the interviews and writings of Msgr. Zanic, one sees other obsessions flow.

Lies

Lies constitute the constant fabric of the accusations which Msgr. Zanic bears against the visionaries and his adversaries. But, if one must call lies the silence and embarrassing or diplomatic words of which he makes crimes, his pamphlet abounds in words of this kind and well illustrates the famous proverb which served as a quotation to this English crown: "Evil be to him who thinks evil," a proverb which unmasks the tendency of each one to accuse his adversaries—of his own faults.

Power

In his pamphlet, Msgr. Zanic attributes to Tomislav Vlasic, and his adversaries, great power of which he would be victim.

But in reverse it is he who holds immense power. As bishop, he has always been protected from on high and supported for a long time in his hard line. But the priests of the parish, who have submitted their grave problems of conscience to the seven major organizations of the Holy See, on March 25, 1985, never received an answer.

The Devil

The devil appears especially in the interviews of Msgr. Zanic; he approves this hypothesis of Michel de la Trinite in the interview with Irish television:

> *Msgr. Zanic:* Five months after the beginning of the apparitions, a psychiatrist from Munich wrote to us: "Everything that I have read on Medjugorje is the work of the devil. The devil wants to gather here large masses of people in order to deliver a terrible blow to the Church." I do not believe that the visionaries have Satan before them, but it is true that there is an intervention from the devil.

Msgr. Zanic presents Medjugorje as a fanaticism, but the parish has perfectly respected him, even during the heated sermon (which hurt many people), which he gave in Medjugorje, against Medjugorje. No parishioner reacted harshly. Respect and prayer overcame everything.

One would be able to answer with a parable. In Medjugorje thousands of pilgrims necessarily leave garbage and refuse. They are not angels. Oberto, a drug addict converted in Medjugorje, devotes his life to picking up the garbage which the pilgrims leave on the two hills: Podbrdo and Krizevac. He cleans up these hills from the daily refuge after he had purified himself from drugs by giving himself over to prayer and to the life of a hermit. Oberto collects the garbage, carts it away and burns this refuse.

The polemic method of Msgr. Zanic begins in the same way but ends the wrong way. He is looking for the "dirtiness," as he calls them. For that he has the zeal of Oberto, who discovers debris even underneath the rocks where the pilgrims hide them, but instead of making them disappear, Msgr. Zanic exposes them in the international press. Indeed, even on the altar, for his episcopal sermon at the Confirmation of July 25, 1987 in Medjugorje, was devoted not to the Holy Spirit, but to the systematic demolition of Medjugorje.

May we know how to look at the beautiful hills of Medjugorje in their savage beauty, the prayers and conversions, the healings and the holiness, the flow of graces which descends from Heaven on these places, and let us leave to the flies their polarization on the garbage.

In support of this parable I have first of all the pleasure to be able to quote Msgr. Zanic. If at the beginning of his polemic writing, he takes upon himself the responsibility to spread evil, at the end, he adopts an opposite solution:

—"I have received letters filled with grave offenses which it is not possible to publish."

When one says something evil about him, Msgr. Zanic understands that it is not necessary to publish it. May he apply that to the rest.

Let us give him this homage, for he is progressing on this point. At the time of Confirmation in 1990 in Medjugorje, on the discreet entreaty which Fr. Orec addressed to him before his visit, he refused to return to his polemics. As bishop, he spoke of the Holy Spirit and the Sacrament which he distributed to the faithful. That closes this chapter in his honor.

SEMIOTIC ANALYSIS OF THE GAINS OF
MSGR. ZANIC AGAINST MEDJUGORJE

A Polemic Structure: Lie—Truth

In order to better understand a writing, it is useful to conduct a semiotic analysis of the contrasting fundamental concept which underlies all discourse. Every concept includes four contrasting aspects: two opposites and their respective contradictory, from which the discourse covers the axis.

The semiotic analysis of the writing of Msgr. Zanic resolves itself in a simple and clear-cut schema like every well established polemic: The good people (Msgr. Zanic) and the bad people. Truth and lies are opposed there with blinding evidence:

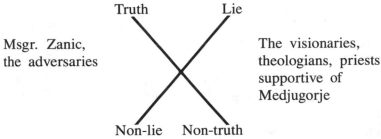

Msgr. Zanic exploits a noble topic: to defend the truth against lies. He attributes to himself the honorable role. According to his speech, the lies are Medjugorje, the visionaries, the Franciscans, their supporters, and the devil. The truth is he himself and the adversaries of Medjugorje, whom he has documented and encouraged. Curiously, Msgr. Zanic ignores their differences because Gramaglia, Belanger, Sivric, and Jones are extremely different and often contradictory among themselves. They find themselves within a broad spectrum which goes from unbelief to traditionalism; from the left to the right, and their struggle against Medjugorje is dictated by reasons which are opposing in some respects, according to the analysis which I have published in *Seven Years* and *Eight Years* (no.

7 and 8), later developed at the University of Notre Dame (USA), on Pentecost, 1989.

In order not to compromise himself with those whom the Pope has excommunicated, Msgr. Zanic does not quote the writings of Michel de la Trinite. But in the televised interview with Kieron Wood for Irish radio-television, he clearly stated his agreement:

> *Msgr. Zanic:* Michel de la Trinite, French, is an extremist of the right but he has written very well of Medjugorje.
> *Kieron Wood:* Very well?
> *Msgr. Zanic:* Very well.
> *Kieron Wood:* Did he not make any errors?
> *Msgr. Zanic:* No, no! I did not write to him. I did not want to correspond with them (Catholic Counter-Reformation) because they are extremists. They are against the Pope. But they sent me everything that they have written.

Msgr. Zanic brilliantly exploits his schema by crediting with the truth, all these adversaries of Medjugorje, and attributing lies to its supporters...

The weak point of this coherent system is that in order to establish the lies of his adversaries, Msgr. Zanic extrapolates and distorts them. He himself fabricates lies and errors which he attributes to his adversaries. In doing this, he damages his own reputation while thinking that he is damaging the reputation of others.

(For this information, see the notes and documents, p. 212-219).

That is only one example. I have pointed out others in the notes. I did not bring out everything because the notes would have then been very difficult to digest and longer than the text, which had taken on an aspect of mockery, uncompatible with the respect due the person and the function of Msgr. Zanic. The dynamics of his text holds two very simple routes:

—Franciscans, visionaries, and supporters of Medjugorje cultivate lies and untruths. They are silent about the truth and invent lies. All the cures (even those which have been recognized by serious investigations) are inventions. They would be the work of Tomislav Vlasic and the Franciscans, etc.

—Msgr. Zanic and the adversaries of the apparitions play the beautiful role of fighting against lies and reestablishing the truth.

St. James Church—Medjugorje

Chapter 5

FRUITS

The fruits continue at Medjugorje, and that is the principal criterion.

1. THE VISIONARIES

The visionaries hold their course, however filled with traps it may be, with the innumerable harassing visits which must unbalance or exhaust them. Three of them have divided their time between a project to fulfill a religious vocation, and this daily service of testimony without speaking of the incidents and personal concerns of each one. They remain simple, sincere, disinterested, credible, and alive: their faith and their love grows deeper. They are accomplishing their mission well, as our chapter 2 permits one to see. The hand of Our Lady leads them.

2. THE NEW COMMUNITIES

Some religious communities were born in 1988, in order to accomplish the program expressed by Our Lady in Medjugorje. They are communities founded on the model of the primitive church and of Pentecost: Men and women open to the breath of the Holy Spirit and its gifts. For some the way was paved with obstacles, as we discussed in our previous two books (*Seven years* and *Eight Years*).

A. The Radical and Opposing Way of T. Vlasic

According to the wishes of the Franciscan authorities, the community of Tomislav Vlasic returned to Yugoslavia, an area close to Medjugorje. Its members discreetly attended the evening liturgy. Their return was a good thing because this young elite group from Medjugorje belongs in Croatia rather than in exile. But Tomislav Vlasic is the number one target of the bishop. It was in the spirit of peace that he had established his community far from the diocese. His return created a problem again.

On the other hand, the mixed character of the community, its novelty, presented embarrassing questions. When the visionary Maria questioned the oracles of Agnes Heupel which guided the community, it created another problem *(Eight Years)*. And so at the beginning of 1990, Tomislav Vlasic was invited to a waiting solution. His community was practically dissolved. Some members, who wanted to lead a community life, were entrusted to Fr. Pancrazio, a Capuchin, near Bari in Italy, while others returned to an ordinary life while continuing to live their commitments. Tomislav Vlasic received this series of blows and disappointments in a profound spirit of peace, humility, and spiritual depth, which impressed me. Many young people are waiting for its renewal in order to enter into his community.

Tomislav chose the straight and narrow way: a contemplative life with a total gift oriented toward a victim offering in union with the Cross of Christ for the redemption of the world. It is a formidable choice, an exceptional way, founded on the Cross of Christ which is the very center of His life and His mystery. Jesus invites His disciples on this road: *"He who wishes to come after Me, let him renounce himself, carry his cross, and follow Me."* (*Mk.* 8:34, *Matt.* 10:38, *Lk.* 9:23).

This austere teaching has always been understood in the Church. In the nineteenth century, many orders of victims were born, principally the Victims of the Heart of Jesus (today the Daughters of the Heart of Jesus, founded by Mother Mary of Jesus Deluil-Martiny (1841-1884). Her vocation of sacrifice was followed to the letter. She died, savagely assassinated by the anarchist Louis Schave, on February 27, 1884. Her cause for canonization had been held up for a long time. Her attraction for the "priesthood of the Blessed Virgin" which she supported in a prudent and generous sense, had been offending (R. Laurentin: *Marie, l'Eglise et le sacerdoce*, Paris 1952, p. 422-480). Today the obstacle does not exist. Pope John Paul II has just beatified her (1990).

Tomislav Vlasic then made a heroic choice in confirmity with the tradition of the Church. The problem was that the choice was for the community, and this extreme commitment would be presumptuous if it did not come from a free movement of God, and it was thus that he succeeded among certain mystics. In summary, it is legitimate to follow Christ up to "the greatest test of love" which is to give one's life freely, without restriction and without bitterness. That is a mystical form of Christian martyrdom.

Tomislav Vlasic, very respectful of the freedoms of men in all circumstances, proposes this warning to evangelical radicalism but does not order it or force it. It will be important for him to watch over it with discernment. On this way, one must guard against every presumption and to be aware of the deep movements of Divine Love. One must protect himself against the excesses of certain zealous priests of the nineteenth century, who systematically "recruited" victim souls without sufficient discernment. It is not necessary to tempt God nor to presume oneself.

Tomislav Vlasic has well demonstrated the height and the depth of his views in response to questions from a prayer group formed by young, very fervent Italians:
—"Sometimes you have spoken of voluntary victims. What does that mean exactly," they asked.

And he answered: "The voluntary victims are the last step of the program of Our Lady. It is the supreme degree of love toward God and toward our neighbor—to give everything to God and to give everything for one's brother, in preparing oneself to suffer, to take upon oneself the aftereffects of sins of his brothers in order to save the world."

Tomislav judiciously places this total gift, this transfer of the sins of the world, on the love of reparation. It is the last step, the supreme gift, which presupposes a purification and a growth in love among those who really become in love with God.

"As the mother is ready to watch all night in order to caress her child, so the persons who offer themselves unite themselves to God, and then there is nothing more in them except love. The mother does not suffer in her heart when she helps her little one, even if she has to stay awake all night. She is happy when she sees her baby happy with her. In the souls who offer themselves, there is this love. The Blessed Virgin wants to develop this love so that difficulties and sufferings are no longer sufferings. It is always a road to the resurrection, and to the extent that we are ready to take upon ourselves the sufferings of Christ and of our brothers, to that extent we experience this love in us. Thus the sins of our brothers are burned in us. The Blessed Virgin wishes for people in these communities to live this love above all among themselves, then for the salvation of the world. (T. Vlasic, in *Eco* 1989, no. 67, p. 5).

Such is indeed the experience of the saints (in Medjugorje, that of Vicka, from whom pain never deprived her of her energy or her smile). Yet, the maxim: "With love, sufferings are no longer sufferings," calls for the least of nuances because sufferings remain: those of Christ crucified, those of Mary on Calvary did not disappear at all but were taken up by the peace of the depths.

Grignion de Montfort, who had a vocation of exceptional suffering, said with the humor which is appropriate to Christian suffering: "Love does not eliminate suffering but sweetens some of its bitterness like sugar makes bitter fruits delicious." (*True Devotion,* no. 154, *Complete Works,* p. 584.)

Thus the Blessed Virgin pleasantly called them "the sweetness of the crosses" (ibid, no. 154). Such was her profound experience. Grignion states:

"I am happy and joyful in the midst of all my sufferings. I do not think there is in the world anything sweeter for me than the most bitter cross when it is steeped into the blood of Jesus Crucified and in the milk of His divine mother. . .I have never made any conversions except after the bloodiest and most unjust interdicts." (Letter 26, *Complete Works,* p. 65.)

Grignion's friends were surprised to see him joyful and without bitterness in the most annoying contradictions. He loved redemptive suffering for Christ so much that he became ill at ease when his missions succeeded so well. His friends rejoiced over them. But he protested:
—"No cross, what a cross!"

Crosses have never failed and will never fail Tomislav Vlasic and his community: attacks from Bishop Zanic, humble and austere departure for a year in the desert, public opposition from Maria (who was the most beautiful flower shaped ornament in his community), multiple difficulties, and dispersion of those whom he had brought together.

But Tomislav Vlasic is ready for everything. He stays in the background and takes up the current impasse in peace. Can his radical way with vows be that of a lay community? Should it not be that of a religious institute? But the rules imposed on religious institutes do not authorize the mixture of both sexes. If he founds this new religious family, can he remain Franciscan? And is it not dangerous for this community to be mixed at a time when even the distance between the two "Abbeys of Bec," men and women, had not prevented a bad situation? The ways of fervor are difficult and laid with traps. How does one reconcile them with prudence?

B. The Oasis of Peace of Don Gianni Sgreva

The other community established to live the message of Our Lady of Medjugorje, "The Oasis of Peace," progresses harmoniously in spite of many difficulties and transfers. It is also a mixed lay community professing the vows of a radical gift. It was founded at Priabona, in the diocese of Vicenza. Its founder, Fr. Gianni Sgreva, a Passionist, theologian and spiritual man, had received a good reception from his superiors, then from Cardinal Ratzinger and from John Paul II himself, who had given him his blessing. The bishop of Vicenza had also welcomed him favorably and had placed a church and a large house at his disposal.

Everything began with a great spiritual momentum, austere and joyful according to the program. But in 1989, a new bishop was named. He rejected this community and had the church closed. The door was closed to every dialogue. It was necessary to leave.

A second bishop welcomed the community wholeheartedly. He visited it frequently. But having seen the tragic lack of priests, he tried to use this flow of vocations to fill the vacancies. It was a good plan, but not for a contemplative community, founded for another reason. The vocations, which flowed more than one could receive, were oriented in another sense.

An unbearable tension, which required a new transfer, resulted from it. Don Gianni Sgreva found sympathy in one of the dioceses of the Pope: Sabina Mirteto, 60 kilometers from Rome, with Msgr. Nicola Rotuno (Italy). This bishop had been a Nuncio in Syria, where he had welcomed the graces and stigmata of Myrna.

A grandiose project was born in Sabina. The community is in the process of buying a large piece of land. The buildings will be constructed in a functional and symbolic manner according to the objectives and goals of the community. According to the program of Don Gianni, the architect, Patrizio Battecletti, had designed a beautiful circular plan which expresses the purpose of the Oasis. In the center, the little circle of 12 houses of the community is closed by the church. In the midst of this circle are a fountain and the statue of Mary, the inspirer of this new religious family.

Surrounding the first circle, a larger ring of 24 houses has been designed for guests and students who will be received for their spiritual formation. In the center, two other structures will form with the letter M (the initial of Mary) the word MIR: peace in Croatian, the key word of the message of Our Lady.

The community presently numbers more than 40 members. Many others attend. Thirteen professed have already made their vows.

The Oasis of Peace has also assumed responsibility for the sanctuary of the Virgin Punta Sebera in the diocese of Iglesias, the province of Cagliari in Sardinia. It has established there a reception center where four or five priests take turns each month while waiting to form a stable community. It is a mixed community formed with men and women, priests, but particularly laymen: some married, but mostly celibate. Their goal is to live the message of Medjugorje with the three religious vows: poverty, chastity, obedience.

The second vow is lived in two different ways, by the celibates and the married people, for chastity does not mean celibate, but order and rectitude in sexuality; good use of marriage for some, abstention in view of the Kingdom for the others. The axis and aims are the contemplative life, prayer, intercession, and hospitality for a spiritual formation according to contemporary culture.

This lay community develops three charisms:
1. Intercession, for all of mankind and for peace which is the purpose of the fourth vow;
2. Expiation with Jesus, the sacrifical Lamb;
3. Reception.

The proximity of Rome permits the students to attend the Salesian University in the suburbs of Rome and to give the necessary intellectual and spiritual formation to brothers and sisters, including future priests. The person principally responsible is Don Gianni Sgreva, assisted by a vice person and a general council consisting of six members, men and women. The development of this community, sprinkled with difficulties, is studded with acts of mortification.

In February 1990, at the "Center of Fasting Prasura" (Arose, Switzerland), I met with Fr. Paul Egli, in the course of a prolonged fast. He told me of a surprising series of little providential signs which led him to the Oasis where he is today spiritual director. When he had reached 60, after having served the missions in Africa, he was looking for a community life in the service of Mary. With this end in view, he made a novena to St. Joseph from March 9-18, 1988 (vigil of his feast). He then providentially found a replacement for his parish; thus he was able to leave on the nineteenth, for his thirtieth pilgrimage to Medjugorje. From Lausanne, he took the train, the Orient Express, to Belgrade. But in Vicenza (Italy), he became sick. He had to get off. There he heard talk about the community of G. Sgreva, then in Priabona. A bus left exactly for that destination a few minutes later, about 7:30 in the morning. He took it. He was welcomed like the Messiah because the community, on its part, was making a novena in order to find a priest to help Gianni Sgreva to direct so many vocations. For that, it was necessary to have a truly spiritual person who spoke many languages (Paul Egli knew some 10 of them, including Croatian). Finally, it was necessary to have a priest devoted to Our Lady and fervent on Medjugorje. Paul Egli fulfilled all of these conditions. He responded to the description which provided for the desires entrusted to St. Joseph. Thus he became the spiritual assisant of Gianni Sgreva at the Oasis.

Following my contact with Paul Egli in the course of his long fast in Switzerland (February-March 1990), I visited the community on May 3-4. Don Gianni Sgreva had me first visit the grounds in the process of being purchased, among the sweet undulations of the neighboring hills, verdant in this springtime. Then we went with the bishop, Msgr. Rotuna, to San Polo, where the community was housed. It is one of those fortified Italian villages built at the top of a hill. (On June 10, 1505, the Blessed Virgin appeared there and gave a message analogous to that of Medjugorje, including fasting on Fridays on bread and water.)

The community numbered 41 members, almost all between 20 and 30 years of age. I appreciated their receptive charisma throughout this day: meals, conversations with the community, then Mass at which I was invited to preach the Gospel of the day. Gianni Sgreva allowed me his room (office) for the siesta and for the short night before my morning departure the next day.

What struck me was the simplicity, the equality, the unity of these 41 young people who belonged to 10 nationalities, men and women. They live heroic lives of discomfort, three or four to a room, respecting the silence of curfew while patiently waiting for the Oasis to be built. Their day? Rising is at 5 o'clock—a long time in prayer and then breakfast. At 8 o'clock the students leave each morning in the minibus for the Salesian University. On the road they recite the first two Mysteries of the Rosary; on their arrival, they recite the office in the chapel.

In the evening, on their return, they say the third Mystery of the Rosary in the minibus. Bedtime at 9:30 p.m.; 10 o'clock in the event of a procession (during the whole month of May) or in several other circumstances. The community reflects a simple, calm, relaxed joy, a true welcoming peace, harmonious prayer, good communication. One of its members explained to me how he used to previously be so sad. He found joy and learned to smile.

Gianni Sgreva develops their prayer life with one of the members of the community: Arnaldo Rufino, who was at the point of being ordained a priest. He is an older, well trained student of Fr. Marie-Dominique Philippe in Fribourg.

On Monday evening there is supplementary prayer from 9:00 to 10:30; on Friday the Stations of the Cross with the people of the village, from 8:30 to 9:30 p.m. The community maintains perpetual adoration. One sole priest will be on duty the whole night. But he is often accompanied by volunteers.

3. PRAYER GROUPS

The development of prayer groups (worldwide) continues. We do not have any new numbers, but it is most likely in the tens of thousands. These persevering groups are often made up of young people at a high level of fervor. According to a sociological inquiry on this development in Italy, the following progress is reported:

- 1 percent of these groups was born in 1982
- 1 percent in 1983
- 2 percent in 1984
- 6 percent in 1985
- 15 percent in 1986 (88 groups)
- 30 percent in 1987 (93 groups)

For 1988, the number of 15 percent represents only the first months of the year. It is thus a sustained expansion. The listed figures are far from being complete, because these improvised groups do not often have the wish to fill out questionaires.

Three hundred and seven groups responded to the questions of the inquiry in Italy. They result from the following traits: These groups are on a steady increase. Their names are inspired by Medjugorje—"Our Lady of Peace"—and other titles of Mary. They are most often formed by lay people, but with participation (or direction) of priests, including parish priests—7 percent are directed by a parish priest, 21 percent by a priest or religious, the rest (the majority) by lay people.

The priests of the parishes know about 93 percent of the cases; favorable in 64 percent of the cases, tolerant in 24 percent. They participate in 38 percent of the cases.

- 57 percent gather at the church
- 19 percent as a family
- 67 percent meet each week (in the evening after dinner), between one and two hours.

The groups are of different sizes, from a minimum of 3 or 4 to more than 1,000! In Rome, *Pro Fratribus* largely exceeds this number. In Genoa, the group *Regina Pacis* gathers 700 assiduous persons. In Goggi, another group, *Regina Pacis,* gathers 600 people. They comprise men and women, young and old, priests and lay people, from different backgrounds.

During the prayer meeting, 95 percent recite the Rosary or at times, the chaplet; 50 percent read the messages of Our Lady of Medjugorje; 35 percent listen to instructions by a priest. In 37 percent of the cases, Mass is celebrated and in 28 percent Mass is followed by adoration of the Blessed Sacrament.

The total number of Italian groups which were identified at the end of 1987 was 16,932. But this number is not exhaustive and has notably increased since that date.

The vitality of these groups produces large regional or national conferences (especially in the United States), for contacts, information, but especially for prayer.

Thus the University of Notre Dame hosted a conference in 1989, which gathered 7,000 people. The success was such that a similar meeting was organized with the same success in May 1990. I was at both of them. The fervor there was deep and calm. Archbishop Franic was there in 1990. Another American bishop presided over the Mass the first day (Saturday, May 5).

A similar conference, organized in Pittsburgh (5,600 participants), with the participation of the visionaries Ivanka (from Medjugorje) and Julia (from Naju, Korea, a stigmatist) did not reduce the participation at the University of Notre Dame where there had been an equal number of participants, and in spite of the later organization of large similar conferences at the University of Steubenville (July 7-8), Irvine, California (August 11-12).

The prayer groups of the parish of Medjugorje, which began this worldwide movement, continue with fervor. Ivan's group has two meetings each week: on Monday on the Hill of the Apparitions, and on Friday on the Hill of Krizevac. Jelena's and Marijana's little group (some 12 members), guided by locutions from Jesus and Our Lady, meets once a month. The large group where there are some adults, three times a week; on Tuesdays, Thursdays, and Saturdays after the evening Mass for an hour or an hour and a half. There are other groups. Jelena's father participates in a new group which was founded in 1989.

It is there that the worldwide movement of prayer groups started. It has spread around the world. The good fruit is PRAYER.

4. PARISH LIFE IN MEDJUGORJE

At what stage is the parish now? It thrived like a hyper-fervent lay monastery during the first years, a time of rapid development and persecution. Today, its citizens are caught up in a whirlpool of organization and commerce, which throws the site into confusion, in order to guarantee the services necessary for such a popular place of pilgrimage. It was necessary to accommodate the pilgrims which became more and more numerous. One could not remain indefinitely dealing with solutions of luck or improvisation. Many take this task seriously. The quality of local prayer and of hospitality has contributed very much to the expansion of the place of pilgrimage, and it remains largely supported by those who construct large family boarding houses. If the unflagging rosaries, attendance at daily mass, and fasting are subsiding, a large number of elite maintain an exceptional level. More than one parishioner matches the deep sanctity of the visionaries. This elite, unique in the world, constitutes the profound parish.

They say that Medjugorje is concerned only with prayer and remains foreign to the social and political. That is a superficial criticism. Peace, serenity, apolitical attitude (maintained in spite of local patriotism and the liveliness of Croatian nationalism) have been a powerful factor of reconciliation with the government which was at first fiercely hostile. This peace has lifted a political weight—the reconciliation between the Church and the State; Medjugorje is a forerunner of "perestroika" and the freedoms which have been progressing rapidly in Yugoslavia.

5. BEYOND MEDJUGORJE

Social Initiatives

The visionary Mirjana has often insisted on the care of the poor and of hospitality. On the other hand, Medjugorje has brought about a number of social initiatives: in Brazil the pilgrimages to Medjugorje returned to their country and contributed to the foundation of safe houses and education for children of the streets—vagabonds without family and without education. Similar stories abound in many other countries.

Prayer

Thousands of Medjugorje prayer groups have been founded and prosper throughout the world. Medjugorje is a breeding ground of initiatives to prayer.

Fasting

Another fruit is the rebirth of fasting, which the new *Code of Cannon Law* failed to abolish, and which the Pope symbolically maintained (two days a year with some minimal prescriptions which certainly did not consist of a "fasting" in the proper sense, not even a diet for whomever wanted to use only the rules). Beyond this last symbol, the messages of Our Lady have spread a stricter and more frequent fast: on bread and water once or twice a week among hundreds of thousands of Christians. Some of them have found in it the tradition and the spirit of fasting and they have pressed farther.

René Lejeune, sparked by Medjugorje, began to fast in 1985 following his first pilgrimage. In order to clarify and spread this forgotten Christian custom, he wrote a book based on his own experience, and especially that of Dr. Bauer, founding pioneer of the Center of Fasting at Arosa (Switzerland), *"Fasting: Cure and Feast of Body and Spirit"* (Parvis 1985). This book has achieved immense success. It has been translated into several languages; it aroused a tremendous interest among the Buddhist monks in Viet Nam. Fasting also reveals some ecumenical dimensions.

This coherent and organic effort is of great influence for

the health of body and spirit, for mastery of instincts (nourishment and sexual) and the meaning of peace.

Dr. Myriam Lejeune, daughter of Professor René Lejeune, had accompanied her father to Medjugorje, then to the Prasura Center of Fasting. She was not gifted for fasting like her father, for whom it was truly a feast and a stimulation of body and spirit. While he conducted his second fasting in euphoria, while happily writing his book, she was sad and said to him: "You are in Heaven and I in purgatory." But she persevered with conviction and discovered, in turn, the medical and spiritual value of fasting.

In turn, she founded a program in France, within the framework of the Community of Chemin Neuf: *"Fasting and Prayer,"* whose title speaks well of its objective. She had her first two sessions in May 1990, in Bordeaux and Nice. This initiative is only one example among many others. The formation of an authentic and integral fast has a great future in the Church for the awakening and the perseverance of vocations, very often disturbed or broken because of an insufficient mastery of the desires and instincts.

Our Lady of Medjugorje in Prison

The American, Joe Bertels, had read my book, *Seven Years of Apparitions.* He immediately established contact with the *Oasis of Peace* founded by Gianni Sgreva in Italy. On his return, he visited prisons in New Jersey. The news of the apparition stimulated prayer which was increased to eight hours a day. The movement spread to other prisons. I have received written testimonies of these prisoners whose lives have been changed. Here are some samples:

"My name is J. E., 30 years old, inmate at Southern State Corrections in New Jersey. My conversion began when I met a brother from the rosary group of Mary Queen of Peace in September 1989. . . When I arrived in prison, someone told me of the apparitions of our Mother Mary in Medjugorje [. . .]. That made my ears prick up. The prison chaplain gave me some books, and I learned about the role of Our Lady in sincere conversions. The more I studied, the more I prayed, and the more at peace I became. On May 19, 1990, the group 'Messengers of Mary' visited us. All had been at Medjugorje and testified to it. On that day the Holy Spirit entered into my life with a joyous peace. Now I study Catholic doctrine and I try to live the message of Our Lady. I will soon be baptized in the Catholic Church. I witnessed a spinning of the sun, here at prison, with my friends, and an officer. I hope some day to go to Medjugorje. . ." (July 28, 1990).

* * *

"Although we were baptized, the Church was not a big part of our family of six children, and we were not encouraged to go to Mass. When I was imprisoned in 1985, the Mass was not in my plans. Drugs, women, and money had been my only gods. In 1986, I returned to prison, cursing my bad luck. I was cut off from my family. In June 1990, someone gave me the book *The Queen of Peace Visits Medjugorje.* Having nothing to do, I read the book in its entirety. The messages of the good mother had a very profound effect on me. Christ was no longer the persecutor of my bad luck. I discovered His saving love. That led me to confession and to Mass every week. The Rosary is part of my daily ritual.

"My situation has not changed since my conversion. Material pressures which weigh on my life as a prisoner are always there, and there are some moments when it overwhelms me. But through the messages of the most Blessed Virgin, I can now face life with a better understanding and a peace which I had never before experienced. Now, I believe in my heart that Christ is my Shepherd and that I can have recourse to Him each time that I need Him." (P. K., same prison, July 25, 1990).

*   *   *

"My name is J. T. I am an inmate at Southern State Corrections. This is the way the Good Mother and the apparitions of Medjugorje helped me to change my life. I belonged to a dysfunctional family but I was sent to a Catholic school and I dreamt for a while of becoming a priest. At fifteen I began to drink, then drugs. God was no longer a part of my life. After two marriages outside of the Church and of arrests for acts of violence, I was condemned to prison for fifteen years. And thus it is that a year ago I began to pray, but without commitment to God. And then our Chaplain showed us a film on the apparitions in Medjugorje. I became very emotional to the point of shedding tears. I was happy that the room was dark! The following days I did not speak to anyone (we view the film on a Wednesday). On Sunday I went to Mass and for the first time in my life I really participated in it. The following Wednesday I returned to learn more about Mary and I saw another film on Medjugorje. I received it with the same incomprehensible emotion. I could hardly wait for Saturday to go to confession, and on Sunday I received Jesus. I was a little lost, but I began to say the Rosary and the Chaplain was a good guide for me. He made me understand Mary, and through her I was able to find Jesus again. Mary is so wonderful! I really love her tenderly. It is she who has brought me back to the Church."

"Now I read everything that falls into my hands on that subject and I prepare, full of hope, for a total consecration through her. I would also like to be strong in my faith and my love for her as Louis de Montfort was. My girlfriend is also in prison.

She had been baptized a Catholic but had never had a religious background. After my letters on my return to God and to His good Mother, she began to ask herself questions and to pray. I sent her a Rosary and some books on Medjugorje. Now she says the Rosary and we have postponed our wedding plans until we are sure what it is that Mary expects of us.

"Mary's presence does not leave me. I verify her intercession in many circumstances. I have seen signs in the sun with approximately seven other prisoners of our Rosary group. But the important thing is that now all I want is to do what pleases my heavenly mother and to grow in her grace." (Undated, probably July 1990).

*　　*　　*

Another prisoner, at Melville, sent me a letter of ten pages of which I reproduce only some key sentences. He was also into drugs and was "hospitalized after an overdose."

"I found myself in prison again, shocked and worn out with suffering [. . .]. In January 1989, one Saturday afternoon, I went to the Queen of Peace Rosary group. It was the first time in my life that I said it. Later I never missed it. This way I learned that Our Lady was appearing in a place called Medjugorje. I began to read, to listen, to discuss, to look at video tapes of the event. Little by little my interest grew in order to know more about it concerning her message. I met visitors to the prison who taught me very much about it and they projected peace, a kindness that I wanted very much; my question to those whom I met was always the same:

—'How did you find such peace?' The response was always the same.
—'By following the messages of Our Lady.'

"My conversion took roots, my desire to find peace grew. My knowledge of the Catholic religion also. I discovered the admirable gift of faith which I received from God. From now on this faith is at work. I attend Mass on Saturday and meet with the chaplain of the prison. I began to receive the Holy Eucharist every day because my desire had grown [. . .]. All that led me to the books of Louis-Marie Grignion de Montfort. *True Devotion to Mary* and the Way of the Cross have led me to make the consecration to Jesus through Mary on December 8, 1989. Thus my love for Mary is strengthened, but my love for Jesus has exploded into a greater love and desire to serve God. It is the message of Medjugorje which has led us to pray the Rosary every day for an hour and to study Holy Scripture. My desire to learn the Bible has increased. The same desire for the Catholic doctrine, etc."

[Here he reports the events and signs which were received in his new life: some physical cures in prison, conversions to the Catholic Church, but without exaltation.]

"Here, in prison, I must face many temptations, but I overcome them in living in and for God. One of my faults is human pride, especially to let myself be seen with a Bible or to receive the Eucharist in the presence of other prisoners. This human pride has disappeared. That may seem a very small victory, but for me it is a marvelous grace of God.

"Now I see that my life was wasted before my coming to prison. I do not know how I survived a serious motorcycle accident and an overdose of heroin which had hospitalized me.

"Recently, one of my friends in prison, with whom I worked for a year, died from a heart attack. He dropped dead in place. I immediately thought: 'No

one knows either the day or the hour.' I had never
considered the day nor the hour when Jesus will
return to earth. I began to consider the day and
the hour of my death. Up to that point I had much
to do to study the Bible, the doctrine, and read the
messages of Our Lady in Medjugorje and apply them
to my life. This death made me understand the messages of our mother. Now, on reading Holy Scripture, I understand more clearly the mercy of God,
the love of Jesus for all, why I escaped death and
received the opportunity to repent. Jesus has helped
me to find some good in me, and I believe that
I have a mission to fulfill in this life. I pray to discover what it is, that I am able to find it. My love
grows for my friends. Medjugorje has been my salvation and I thank the most Blessed Mary for having led me to Jesus [...]. I love our Catholic
Church, our Holy Father Pope John Paul II. God
Almighty and Jesus occupy a big place in my heart.

"In March 1989, I obtained from an official, a
room in the prison where we can pray in peace without distractions and in this prayer group we learn
about the apparitions of our Blessed Mary in the
small village of Medjugorje. I found again what I
had learned when I was a child and I love God
with all my heart. Mary has helped me to overcome
my emotions, not to show my resentment against
what I do not like. I offer everything to Mary. In
prayer she frees me from temptations. The two visits
from the 'Messengers of Mary,' who had returned
from Medjugorje, who shared with us their experiences, have been very inspiring for me (for a
discovery of the Holy Spirit). I have turned all my
life to Jesus and Mary in doing total consecration
to Jesus, through Mary, according to Grignion de
Montfort. I have discovered Mary's place in everything. This is the prayer which I have written to her:

To Mary My Mother

Oh, very dear and beloved Mother Mary, show me your very pure heart so that I can imitate you and pray with you each day, now and throughout the rest of my life. May I be able to accept with all my heart every trial and tribulation which could disturb my life [...]. I love you, Mary, my mother, and Jesus, my Lord, with all my heart, soul, body, and spirit. Be with me always." (V. B. P. H., July 28, 1990).

Testimony from a Confessor

Tomislav Vlasic, who hears confessions regularly in Medjugorje, recently said:

"It is enough to enter the confessional in order to believe. It is the true miracle which moves and opens the eyes with respect to the presence of Mary. The indisputable sign which is repeated here each day are the confession-conversions. It suffices to spend several hours in the confessional. In the 'waters' of Medjugorje there are some rare 'large fish,' as there are everywhere. Here the confession-conversion becomes the general rule. So many of those baptized have made confession a rite, or only an enumeration of sins without the commitment which must flow from it. The man who remains here for at least a few days falls on his knees, goes to confession with a great disposition, and accepts to change his life.

"These pilgrims are young, old, or in the prime of life. Their last confession took place 10, 20, 30, indeed 50 years ago. Everything is done without embarrassment, without minimizing or exaggerating their past conduct. They sorrowfully discover what they are, what they would deserve, and how they are freely loved. And when the word of confidence and of mercy from the priest accompanies the hand which rises to absolve them, how many then receive the gift of tears and a true heart of flesh (*Ezech.* 36:26).

"There comes to Medjugorje what comes less and less in the world of today. In all simplicity they confide their most serious problems [. . .]: sharp crises which they live as married couples, families, parishes. . .prisons; others weep and cry for mercy for children who have been aborted. Still others come to offer their accounts of hatred and injustice which paralyze their lives. Some place in Mary's heart an abyss of filth and of misery. There is the drug addict who softens his heart through his poverty, his humility, his resolution to leave it with the help of a community; prostitutes who are determined to become a new family; mothers of abandoned children; the homosexual who brings here other 'suffering brothers' so that mercy may touch them as it touched him. Some receive here the call to a vocation or the confirmation of a call already perceived.

"The confessions which soften the most are those of the young because of their total openness, their sincere repentance, the serious penances which they freely impose upon themselves, their very generous bursts of enthusiasm which grace suggests to them. Msgr. Carboni, Bishop of Masserata, was right when he said: 'When I go to a shrine, I go into the confessional. And by means of this, I can judge the validity of the shrine. I went to Medjugorje. I did not try to see the visionaries. I heard confessions for two whole days, and it was this that made me say that in Medjugorje, the Blessed Virgin is present, and with her, Our Lord.'

"Msgr. Hnilica said in the same way on June 25, 1990: 'In Medjugorje I began to hear confessions five hours during which there were many people waiting. During these five hours, so many penitents came as I have never seen during forty years of my life as priest and bishop. Many would say to me as they genuflected:

—'I do not know how to confess my sins...I came out of curiosity, but I feel that I must make my peace with God and begin again a new life...Help me, what must I do?' "
(Interview recorded by A. Bonifacio)

Chapter 6

TESTIMONIES

1. Conversions

Medjugorje is a place of numerous and deep conversions. *Eco* and other periodicals (English, American) periodically published some of them. Here are two which date from 1984.

From the IRA to the Seminary

The history of the Irish terrorist, Marc Lenaghan, is a response for those who consider the message of Medjugorje like a flight into prayer without any consequences. This member of the IRA (acronym which means wrath) was an unbeliever. It seemed to him that Christians were cowards and traitors. His life was committed to murder and vengeance. This is his testimony:

"It was not our rifle which killed, but our heart. For years I have killed without pity. After each attack, we were sorry that we had not killed more. After the rifle fire of January 15, 1982, in Belfast (False Road), where a soldier who was seriously wounded was left abandoned, I was arrested with a friend in combat and condemned to 12 years in prison. I spent only six years there. Hatred, rancor, and bitterness raged in this prison. Yet all the members of the IRA attended all the Masses which were celebrated for the prisoners. The Mass was for us a means of finding each other, of sharing news of plots and conspiracies. In Easter 1984, I heard for the first time about Medjugorje. The prison chaplain had returned from a pilgrimage. He himself had experienced a conversion there. He spoke enthusiastically of reconciliation with God, of love and of mercy. After Mass I asked him:
—'How can you believe all that?'

70

"For me, it was like a fairy tale, but I would have loved for it to be true. I felt as though crushed, but took up hope again. The chaplain put me in contact with other fellow countrymen, pilgrims to Medjugorje. In a book, I read the beautiful messages of the Gospa, the cures, the conversions. The love of God entered me. Salvation had been possible for all sinners in the Gospel—the tax collector Zacheus, the prostitute Mary Magdalene—why not I?

"Jesus loves every sinner, thus also a terrorist from the IRA. Having been freed in 1988, I went directly to Medjugorje and found the faith there. I did not see the miracle of the sun, I did not have apparitions, but I had a meeting—miraculous. I found myself at the foot of the cross on Mt. Krizevac. A man approached me and said to me:

—'I have heard the story of your life and I would like to speak with you.'

To my great surprise, this man was an English soldier! He asked me:

—'When were you arrested?'

I told him:

—'On February 15, 1982, at the time of an attack on False Road.'

He said to me:

—'I was on patrol there as an English soldier. I remember this attack.'

"How strange the paths of God are! This English solider and I were two of the converts and pilgrims. Many years before, we were face to face in Belfast. I wanted to kill him; he wanted to kill me. And here we are in the process of praying the Rosary together for peace in Ireland."

Conclusion:

1. There is hope for every sinner: the thrower of bombs is preparing himself now for the priesthood in the seminary

in Ireland. The British soldier has been converted also.
2. There is hope for the world. If all the opposing adversaries in so many wars prayed together in Medjugorje as was the case with this magnificent duo, there would be peace everywhere. May God so wish it! (PAV, June 17, 1989, an account recorded by M. Waterinckx).

From Murder to the Priesthood
"My mission will be to cure the wounded"

Fr. Pere Slavko interviewed this revolutionary who became a convert and had him give exact details with respect to his spiritual adventure:
—Where did he come from?
—How was he converted?
—And where is he going now?

Here is the essence of it (*Eco,* no. 71):

Fr. Slavko: Who led you to prison?

R.: I am Irish, a native of West Belfast. My parents and two brothers are there. I did Slavic studies there, specializing in Russian literature and Marxism. I also studied English literature. I was violent. I grew up without faith, without prayer, without any knowledge of God. In 1978 I became a member of the Irish Republican Army. I began to distribute writings and manifestos against the Church, against religion, and against the English. I was a violent person among others.

What led me to prison? My group had attacked a house and took its tenants as hostages [. . .]. When the soldiers arrived, we began to fire on their vehicles, then on the windows of the house. A British soldier was killed. In spite of the curfew, I drove through the city on a motorcycle with a friend, my machine gun on my shoulders. At the very moment when I went to kill a British soldier, the motorcycle overturned. I was captured and arrested while my friend succeeded in escaping. In prison I was subjected to seven days of questioning and condemned to twelve years in prison. I served six years and two months and was freed on condition.

Fr. Slavko: What was your interior disposition?

R.: In my childhood in Belfast, our house had been burned down. A number of my friends and acquaintances had been killed. We accused the British soldiers of it. Rage was ablaze. I lived for vengeance. I hated. So I quickly entered a political organization. They convinced me of the justice of our struggle. Our main idea was this: we are fighting for peace, freedom, and justice. We were driven by hatred, vengeance, exasperation [. . .]. I became a member of the local police of the IRA.

My task was to attack and to strike at what seemed to us dangerous. We struck, wounded; we thought of accomplishing a noble responsibility [. . .]. I knew how to fight. I was courageous. I had acquired the confidence of the highest directors of the IRA. Some qualified specialists taught us how to kill British soldiers and police or other adversaries. The instructor would repeat to us often: "It is not the gun which kills but the heart." I was angry when I did not kill [. . .]. We had no idea about ethics and respect for the life of others. Even in prison I remained the same.

Fr. Slavko: What path led you to Medjugorje?

R.: At the Mass where we went, a missionary spoke to us about the visionaries, the messages, the secrets, the conversions. I said to myself: "This priest believes in it [. . .]." I asked him to explain to me a little better how the Madonna appeared in Medjugorje.

—"I am going to send you some books," he answered.
—"Do not take the trouble; all that does not interest me," I replied.

And yet he sent me some books. I read them all, but I did not accept them. Everything began on Easter 1984. A silent voice began to open my heart. While reading, I stopped at a photo of all the visionaries. It cut my breath; Vicka's smile was for me a proof that it was not a game but a serious matter. This was a seed that was planted in my heart. I accepted the possibility that everything was true [. . .]. I was in conflict with Christianity. Christians seemed to me weak, traitors to our revolution and our struggle. I read again; I reflected [. . .]. I could not pray. I could not, but a choice imposed itself. I had to make decisions between the teachings which the Blessed Virgin offered and all that I had admitted up to that moment as the basis of my life. I stopped rejoicing over murders. Now I became sad when I learned about a murder [. . .]. My friend asked me about these new feelings. I felt that I had to make a choice again: remain in the movement of our army or, indeed, accept the truth of Our Lady and change my life. God was there, present. He acted. I experienced Him. I began to participate at Mass. I went to confession. I received Holy Communion. I stopped going to the army's lessons.

Finally, one day I appeared before the leaders of the IRA and I said to them, "I can no longer morally justify the armed conflict and the assassinations. Life has become for me a value. I can no longer destroy it."

I appeared to them as a traitor and a coward. But from now on it was my way [. . .]. It was difficult for me to believe that God forgave me. The example of David, who had an innocent person killed and whom God forgave, helped me. I thought of St. Paul who had persecuted Christians and became an apostle. I found strength and confidence in the mercy of God. It began in prison. But since then, I have been free and happy [...].

I was freed in August 1988. I came to Medjugorje. There I found the call to joy and love. Previously my love was limited: my parents, the IRA, some friends. In Medjugorje, one single proof was imposing: one has to love each man according to his worth and his own dignity. And it is clear that we are all victims: we from the IRA, and the British soldiers or policemen.

We are victims of passions, violence, and injustice without love. We are victims and not targets on which one must fire. The training of Mary has done this: an incredible change for me [...]. At Easter 1989—my second trip to Medjugorje—I went up to Krizevac and I prayed. A pilgrim who knew the history of my life asked if he could narrate it to another person.
—"Who is that?" I asked him.
—"A British soldier who is here and to whom I would like to tell of your experience."

I agreed. We spoke. It was a soldier who had pursued me when I was arrested. At the end of the conversation, we embraced one another wishing each other peace and to everyone.

Fr. Slavko: And today, what are your plans?

R.: Since my first return to Ireland, I began to work on a spiritual plan and I discovered that my vocation was to cure the wounded. God will profit from my experince to help others. I attained a conversion because three people prayed for me. Our

Lady says that even wars can be stopped through prayer. It is possible, then, if we pray in spite of hatred, violence, and scorn. For that, it is necessary to work very hard, to work as Christians. It is necesary to transform destructive forces into forces of conversion and of construction. This way peace will be truly possible [. . .]. Now I want to become a priest. I have already visited a seminary.

God loves us; He picks us up when we have fallen. He teaches us how to love. I have only one desire: to be a witness of this divine love. (Taken from *Sveta Bastina,* February 1990).

Juliana's Conversion

Juliana Ebert, 44 years of age in 1984, belonged to a family of 14 children. One of her brothers was named Tito. She was Baptist but not a practicing one. She had married a German, Hans Ebert. They lived very near Heidelberg. She was far from being an example of conjugal fidelity. But her husband, a Catholic, had complete trust in God. He told Juliana: "I continue to pray for you, and you will return to me."

On a trip to Belgrade, he succeeded in convincing her to make a detour through Medjugorje. On May 18, 1984, apparently the Blessed Virgin appeared to her in her room. She was there, surrounded by a strong light. She wore a white robe and a blue mantle. She appeared very young, very pure. The apparition lasted only a few minutes. Our Lady was looking at the crucifix above the bed, and that struck Juliana in such a way that she spontaneously began to pray the few prayers that she knew, and the Blessed Virgin prayed with her. Her husband had seen nothing of the apparition. But he saw Juliana who had knelt down, and he experienced an aroma of roses. At that moment, he was freed from an illness from which he suffered up until then. Since that May 18, Juliana's life has completely changed. On Saturday, the nineteenth, she was baptized by Fr. Slavko in the chapel of the church in Medjugorje. Vicka was her godmother.

Juliana spoke with the bishop of Mostar. She could not understand his ill will with respect to Medjugorje, for he had been sensitive to the account of her conversion.

Her husband was very surprised at the change of his spouse: before, it was jewels, makeup. She, who never went to church, now goes every day. (According to *Bildzeitung,* December 14, 1984, and *Frau im Speigel,* April 17, 1986.)

Conversion of a Young Man 19 Years of Age (September 15, 1987)

"Since the age of 14, I drank, did drugs. Since I did not have enough money to do it, I stole. I led this kind of disorderly life for 5 years. At age 19, I realized that this life was not really in keeping with what my parents had taught me and I was also disgusted with it.

"My parents spoke to my sister and me of Medjugorje, the marvelous things which took place there, and even offered to take us on one of these tour groups which they were organizing. But I was not interested. My heart was closed to all propositions of this kind and to the call from God.

"In September 1987, I had the desire to go there but did not know why. A few days before their departure, I told my parents that I would like to go, but they told me it was impossible, that all the places had been sold, that I should have told them before. Since they were in the habit of quoting me some passages of the Lord in all instances, I told them: 'If the Lord wants me to go, I am going to be able to go there.' The next morning, there was a cancellation and I was able to go. Thus the Lord wanted me there.

"On September 12, 1987, the whole family flew off to Yugoslavia. During the bus trip to the airport, I saw that all these people were not of my kind: they prayed, sang to the Lord and the Blessed Virgin. Sitting on the bus, my sister and I rode along, pretending to sleep, telling ourselves: 'On what ship did we embark there?' On the airplane, it went better. They had beer, wine, and hostesses.

"On arriving at the village of Medjugorje, I was immediately struck by its backwardness. A very common village, where one could hardly move by bus, for people were walking freely along the street. I asked my mother, 'What is going on here?' 'The people are coming from Mass,' she answered me.

"I was very surprised about this first contact with Medjugorje. On the morning after, the activities of the pilgrimage began: go to the Hill of the Apparitions, see the visionaries, attend services in church . . . I looked around. I found that the people had a happy air about them. Without embarrassment they walked about, the rosary around their neck or in their hands. They were praying, filled with peace and joy. I saw that there was really something special in Medjugorje. I felt drawn; I experienced like a presence of Love that made me feel happy. I began then to participate in prayer with the group. I did not know all my prayers; I have since learned them. I was following along and I was surprised because it was not so bad for me to join them.

"On the morning of September 15, we left for Mt. Krizevac to make the stations of the cross as a group. At the very bottom, since my parents were the leaders of the group, they said:
—"Those who feel called upon to remove their shoes and offer this penance for the conversion of sinners, listen to your heart!"

"I looked at the mountain and thought: 'But they are fools to climb with bare feet!' Two, three removed their shoes. Surprised, I believed indeed called on, I too removed my shoes thinking that

I had to take advantage of all opportunities so that I would not come this far without doing anything. We began to climb. At each station we stopped. These people prayed; I prayed also. All that they did, I also did.

"Having reached the twelfth station, everyone knelt down. I too knelt down. There I began to cry. I did not know why I was crying. Inwardly, I asked myself: 'What is wrong with me? What is happening to me here? I made it through the other stations and did not cry; why do I cry like a child here?' I did not understand. While I was crying like that, one of the group had a prophesy which said:
—'A person from the group is cured from drugs and from everything which is attached to them, and the Lord gives him a grace of extraordinary conversion.'

"At the moment when these words were said, I experienced a great peace and joy. Immediately I began to thank God. It was truly at this twelfth station that the Lord took possession of me, converted me, changed me completely. I did not realize it at the moment, but because of all that He made me experience following that, I understood the greatness of Jesus Who died on the Cross (Twelfth Station). Jesus has come. He has died to save us from our sins. Beginning with this moment, everything began to come alive in me. I desired with all my heart to follow His commandments, to listen to His voice, pray to Mary, to follow her messages.

"During the pilgrimage, I received the word of the rich young man. I knew that, like he, I had to leave my goods if I wanted to follow God. Not that I was rich, but because they were not good things. Medjugorje was for me a second life. I was born again: my heart renewed itself, my faith also. An unforgettable experience which brought me peace and interior joy.

"My confessions made in Medjugorje have helped me very much; the fact also of feeling surrounded by the presence of Mary, of making me feel loved. I had the feeling that I was important and that I could help the world.

"Upon my return from the trip, it was necessary to do my housekeeping duties with respect to my old life. I quickly realized that it would not be easy. On the morning of my arrival, I went to visit one of my friends. On seeing me enter his house, he fixed his eyes on my cross and my medal which I had around my neck. I saw in his eyes that he knew our friendship was over, for it would be a danger for me to fall. If he so decided, it would be he who would come to my ways. It was a grace, but at the same time, it was a cross. He was my best friend. I loved rock music and heavy metal. . .I had to leave that also. I was going out with a girl and I saw that if I wanted to live according to what the Lord asked of me, I had to leave her also, for I was not able to live in chastity with her. It was another hard blow for me. But I did not have the choice; I felt stopped if I did not do that. It was important for me to live His laws and His Word. 'Blessed are the pure of heart, for they will see God.' I want to see God; thus, it is necessary for my heart to be pure!

"The Lord worked marvels in my life. Here is one. I had never done any professional studies and in the 20 some jobs that I had, I never found what I wanted. The Lord gave me a job which I like very much. I am a sacristan in the church of my parish. I have been there for ten months. Even that is something great, for previously I held a job for only a few weeks. What grace to work in His company, to be near Him.

"These times, by stages of discernment, I try to know my vocation. A priest? A brother? The married life? What is His will concerning me? I know that where He wants me, it is there that I will be the happiest. I always pray that I keep persevering in His ways. When I make a mistake, with His grace I get up again. I thank Him before you for what He has done and will do for me. Amen! Alleluia!" (Source: *Messages,* July 1990)

Christine's Conversion (1987)

"It was Palm Sunday, 1987, that I came for the first time to Medjugorje. For some months I had refused the invitations. Being an atheist, I regarded the apparitions of the Blessed Virgin as fundamentally impossible. On setting out three weeks later, on this trip which had been foreseen only for a week, I had only one desire: to attach myself to Mary like a little child so that she might lead me closer to Jesus. My family was Catholic, but I had progressively moved away from God and the church since my childhood. At the age of 14, I chose a non-religious education; I refused to go to church on Sunday. Naturally, I did not pray anymore and did not go to confession.

"Then I entered into a long period of rebellion during which I looked for what I thought was freedom and self-determination. I no longer wanted to recognize any authority; that seemed a constraint to me. I took the word 'freedom' as an opening to all experiences and I believed everything was permitted: atheistic or anarchical books, sex, alcohol, pubs, discotheques, everything. I regarded God as an invention and I resented the human condition as fundamentally absurd (cf. Sartre). To me, people seemed naive, manipulated, repugnant, superficial and cynical. I saw only myself; I evolved more and more in that direction. My habitual reactions were aversion, disdain, criticism, and self-destruction. In spite of all the distractions of nightlife, alcohol, drugs, cinema, theater, my soul was empty and hungered for love. I did not know what I now know— that the love much sought after could not be found in this world, but only in God. I was free then, near despair; I did not know peace of the heart. Such was my life a year ago. I am now going to narrate my radical change."

"In 1985, my father had the opportunity to hear someone speak about Medjugorje, and he went there the same year. He returned full of enthusiasm. The following year all the other members of our family went, except me, in spite of all the invitations to go. At that time, I was no longer living with my parents and sometimes I reacted in a very aggressive way when I heard talk of the apparitions of the Blessed Virgin. But usually I was happy to joke about it. At that time, my parents' attitude changed. They were more open to my considerations; they reproached me less, even when I was disagreeable and sulky. For the first time, I felt that they accepted me as I was. In spite of that, I was far from being interested in Medjugorje. Nevertheless, I also became more tolerable. I thought, 'Perhaps it is a good movement, but my place is not with Catholics.'

"I continued to lead the same life as before, but perhaps with more problems. In 1987, two days before Palm Sunday, my mother went to Medjugorje, I refused to accompany them although I was on vacation. It was as if I had something to lose at Medjugorje, something that I did not want to give up. But my mother had hardly left, when I became ill. I felt sorry that I had not gone with her. The next morning, through the prayers of my brother and father, I found myself seated on the train, traveling south.

"After a trip of thirty hours, I arrived in Medjugorje. The evening Mass was drawing to a close. I felt rather irritated to find myself finally at this place which I did not want to visit. While I was looking for the address of my family, I met Fr. Pero. He drove me in his car to find my mother; he asked me what had led me to Medjugorje. I answered him with irritation:

—'I do not know myself why I am here; I am not interested in the apparitions of Mary; I do not even believe in God.'

"Then Fr. Pero's face lit up and he said, 'I am happy that you are here; the Mother of God will do the rest.' I was totally upset.

"When my mother saw me, she was surprised. The first days in Medjugorje were terrible for me. I walked here and there on the hills thinking to myself: 'Astonished with this marvelous landscape, people come to the idea that God has created it!' And not knowing what else to do, I went to Mass in the evening. It was tortuous for me. Like many others who could not find a seat inside the crammed church, I sat on the ground among the believers.

"I felt like a traitor, a leper. Did I not believe that God was an invention of man? At the same time I was sorry not to be like they—full of love and of peace. My sadness was unfathomable [. . .]. On Thursday after the evening Mass, my mother asked me to come into the side chapel for the adoration of the Most Blessed Sacrament. Since I did not want to return to the house all alone, I accepted. Prior to that moment, I would not kneel down for all the gold in the world, and, behold, I fell on my knees.

"It is still difficult for me to explain what happened to me then. Our German language group sang the *Sanctus* of Schubert with a priest and suddenly I believed. I do not see how to better describe this moment. Between the moment before and the latter, I began to believe that God existed and that He became Man, that He had taken the form of bread and was present there in the Sacred Host. I wept.

"The following days I wept often, but at the same time I experienced the merciful love of God. On Holy Thursday I made my confession, and then for the first time in my life, I was able to celebrate Easter appropriately. I had been raised from the dead. After Easter, I remained two weeks longer in Medjugorje, alone, without my family. Now I was able to accept in my heart the fact of the apparitions and all that Our Lady said. I realized that she was my very loving mother and took me by the hand and that she was always at my side with her smile. It was an experience of happiness for months when I heard Mass, when I prayed, when I would say the names of Jesus and of Mary, or simply when I thought about them.

"Since that time my life has changed completely, in a manner in which I would have never imagined. I stopped smoking, drinking, listening to degrading music. Again I had become a joyful person. The Mass was the highlight of my day, and I was extremely happy that the King of kings came into my heart in Holy Communion in order to give His love to me and through me, to all those whom I would meet. I strongly believe that God will continue to guide me through Mary. Where will He lead me?

Note: (Christine now lives in a community established in the service of "Jesus through Mary" in

order to live her messages of peace. She has consecrated her life to God, hoping through her acts
of reparation, to accomplish the grace of conversion for sinners, this grace which she has herself
received through the prayers of others.)

A New Life for the Singer Lola Falana

In April 1989, Lola Falana went to Medjugorje, dressed
in a white tunic. She prayed with Maria at the site of the
first apparitions. She said:
—"In coming to Medjugorje, I have realized the greatest dream
of my life. I have decided to spend some months each year
in this holy place. All that I have lived this week has been
marvelous."

It was the aftermath of her cure from multiple sclerosis,
of which she has testified in a church in Chicago, before 3,500
people.

"Consequently," she said, "I will go to Medjugorje. I will be Vicka's guest for a week; I will
live some days near this marvelous girl in order
to learn from her the immense joy which a human
being experiences when he enters into contact with
the mysterious world of the beyond, of God. My
trip to Medjugorje is not a tourist trip or one of
curiosity; it is a pilgrimage. I did not know anything about Medjugorje, but I was sick, restricted
to a wheelchair by multiple sclerosis. I saw on television a documentary about the Yugoslav apparitions, which lasted two hours, and I followed it with
the liveliest participation. When the television
showed the crowd of pilgrims which ascend the Hill
of Apparitions, I experienced a great desire to go
there, to walk with them, but my legs were inert,
dead. I tried to move them, but for a long time
they did not respond any longer to the command
of my brain. Then, with tears in my eyes, I prayed

to the Blessed Virgin to help me, promising her that if one day I would be able to walk again, I would go there. As everyone knows now, God cured me of multiple sclerosis and now I am able to realize my promise to find Our Lady in Medjugorje."

The singer is now 47. To the questions of journalists who asked concerning her plans, she answered:

"From now on, I consecrate myself completely to God."

"Are you going to be a religious?" they asked.

"The Lord has not given me the vocation to enter a convent. He has made me understand that I am to stay in the world, in the midst of these people who for years have admired me as singer, dancer, and actress. My role now is to make God and His immense goodness known. And for that I will go to speak about my experiences and my cure obtained by faith, wherever they will invite me, in the churches, in the universities, in the religious communities, on television.

"In that regard, my life will be similar to that of nuns. Like them, I will consecrate all my time exclusively to the Lord. I will observe absolute chastity; I will become disinterested in money; I will always keep this white, very simple dress which I designed and which is a symbol of the mission which I hope to fulfill." (Lola Falana, Las Vegas; translated from *Medjugorje Torino,* June, 1990.)

Conversion of an English Agnostic

Bernard Ellis, a Jewish Englishman, discovered Medjugorje during his vacation in 1983 in Yugoslavia with his family. He was struck by the warm hospitality received and the atmosphere of holiness, of peace, of friendship. He returned there twenty times.

"For me," he said, "it is better to go to Medjugorje for my physical rest and spiritual healing, than to go on vacation anywhere else."

He reached the conviction that Mary was appearing.

"One day," he said, "I was at the Friday night apparition on the hill of Kirzevac. I found myself right next to Maria at the moment when the apparition began. Someone asked me to announce it so that there would be silence and all would fall on their knees. I did it and I knelt down for the first time in my life."

In 1989, during the adoration of the Blessed Sacrament, he accepted the real presence of Christ in the Eucharist and the mystery of the Trinity. A month later, Fr. Jozo Zovko prayed over him, and he decided to become Catholic. Fr. Richard Foley, S.J., has recorded his testimony which we summarized here. (*Medjugorje Messenger,* January-March, 1990.)

2. Letters Received

Here are some testimonies picked at random from letters and communications received:

"I feel the responsibility of asking, in the name of the pilgrims from Venice (region where the bishop restrained the pilgrimages according to requests from the Bishop of Mostar), that the time when the Church will approve the apparitions of the Blessed Virgin be accelerated. Medjugorje is a reality which we cannot ignore. Only the will of God can realize these true baths of spirituality, of simplicity, and of humility. Many of those who go there change their way of life. They find prayer again while listening to the messages from Heaven. The deepest message is the presence of the Madonna. The light of her love imposes itself. She guides toward conversion and reconciliation. Why smother this cry from Heaven?" (Letter from Mariano Spezzapria to Cardinal Ratzinger, dated July 3, 1986.)

*　　　*　　　*

"The Bible speaks of the signs of the times. Could this be the time of the signs?" (Frs. Aloys and Gerald Held, OFM, Cincinnati, USA, November 1988.)

*   *   *

"For a very long time, I have wanted to write to you to thank you for your marvelous book *Messages and Teachings of Mary at Medjugorje*. I think that if it were necessary, I would sell everything in order to get me one. I recommend it very highly. I have just received *Eight Years,* and I am happy to have news from there. Medjugorje is an open door to Heaven. (C.R. to La N., November 10, 1989.)

*   *   *

The Medjugorje Star of June 1989 gives a long testimony about Sister Mary Grace Danos (May 2, 1915-June 12, 1989). In the evening of her life, she discovered Medjugorje in November 1986 (she had just celebrated her seventieth birthday). A fall which had occurred in the preceding months had broken her shoulder. They tried to repair it with surgical grafts, but a graft had been rejected, and the least movement of the arm caused pain.

"Our group was going to laboriously climb Krizevac, when Sister Mary Grace received a cure from her pains. How happy she was to be able to raise her two arms during the last Mass in praise to God for her cure!"

After this first pilgrimage, Sister came to Medjugorje eleven times. Several times she stayed there a month in order to influence other groups. She sent 5,318 pilgrims there, 136 priests, and a bishop, in less than 3 years. (According to Kay Mule, in *The Medjugorje Star,* 3, June 1989.)

*   *   *

"I was truly touched by the message of our mother, the Virgin Mary. I love her and would like to know more about the apparitions of Medjugorje to strengthen my faith." (M.M.K., at Malaoui, September 29, 1989.)

∗   ∗   ∗

One day in Medjugorje, 2,000 kilometers from here, everything went topsy-turvey; everything in my life took on a new dimension before the cross of Krizevac, up there on the mountain. Thank you, my God, at last I have found You!

For nearly six years, as the Blessed Virgin requests, I have gone to confession every month. It was difficult at first. I had to decide each month that it was necessary to persevere. Little by little the need to go to confession came to me, and then the sudden awareness that God speaks to me through this sacrament of His goodness without limit. Now each one of my confessions has become a process of the heart, a sweet meeting. (Stephanie, in *News From Medjugorje,* October 1989.)

∗   ∗   ∗

I used to flatter myself by not going to confession with my "grocery list." My examination of conscience was more of an introspection (turned to me) than a conversion (turned to God). Confession should have humiliated me because I fell again unceasingly in the same sins and that made me feel guilty. It is in Medjugorje that my opinion about this sacrament of pardon changed. Before Apparition Hill, I brusquely stopped in anguish: My God, why did I come here; because of a physical handicap, I cannot climb up?

Immediately a man approached me and presented me with a beautiful small box: "It is a relic of Little Therese," he said. "It was she who said: 'May each of my difficult steps make a missionary priest take a step!' "

On hearing that, I was as though seized by a fire which moved me forward: take one, two, three steps. . .what does it matter if I fall, at least my life would have yielded some fruit. Now, five years later, I do not know what happened to me then. The fact is that I climbed Podbrdo as though I had been carried.

But it is not what happened to my body that was most important; I experienced concretely the answer from God to my interior cry: My God, why have You called me to Your following? Do You not see that I am handicapped of heart and unusable?

God made me understand that in allowing oneself to be carried by Him and His saints, one can go very far. It is nothing then to be handicapped; on the contrary, it will permit Him to intervene. It is undoubtedly because of it that the handicapped have a privileged place in the heart of God. At that moment, I understood my sin: In my handicaps, I did not allow myself to be seen by God.
—I prevented Him from helping me, from loving me and curing me.
—I contributed to the greatest suffering of God. It was as if I "saw" the Lord before me, His arms filled with gifts, telling me after so many and so many times: "Take, do not cry any more," and I saw myself lament over my miseries without acknowledging His love, and in reproaching Him with indifference. Sorrowfully, I became aware that it was crucifying Him again. On that day, I ran to a priest and said, "I do not have the true faith, my Lord and my God, forgive!"

Beginning with that moment, slowly, I began to convert myself and to note: the most beautiful gift which God has left us is His Spirit. I wasted 70 times 7 times a day, and because of that, I need God's forgiveness each day. (U.T.)

* * *

I have just read your book, *Messages and Teachings of Mary at Medjugorje*. It has given me much hope in this world where violence and the degradation of the human being reign. I love very much our Holy Mother of God and wish to read more about her... (Madame H., November 6, 1989.)

* * *

It was in the spring of 1986 that I read your first book on Medjugorje. I had obtained it through curiosity, and it was thus that I was born again. Later I read *Messages and Teachings of Mary at Medjugorje* and I live them as well as I can. Your book gave me a deeper understanding. (F. I., Maryland, USA.)

* * *

We went to Medjugorje on May 13, 1989, for Pentecost: a pilgrimage which had been organized after our recent conversion [...]. In Medjugorje we found consolation, peace, serenity, and a response to our situation (bereavement). And I received in my heart the request of the Most Blessed Virgin to pray the Rosary; that is what I have organized since my return. And then we have at the house every Thursday evening, a prayer meeting where we offer 15 to 18 rosaries to the Lord. But I want at all costs to make Medjugorje known to as many people as possible. (Mr. and Mrs. H., Belgium.)

*   *   *

I have not stepped inside a church for some twenty years (I am 38), except for family ceremonies. I read a book about Medjugorje, and after a year, I did not fail to participate in Mass on Sundays and feast days. I make every effort, with more or less success, to obey Mary in my daily routine, on all the points which she clearly gives in Medjugorje. That is all. Nothing spectacular. (M. T., in M., December 5, 1989).

*   *   *

Many letters report cures. One of them came from a priest who counseled a mixed marrige of over ten years—he an Algerian Muslim, she French. This priest gave them two audio cassettes on Medjugorje: one of Sister Emmanuel, and the one which I had recorded three years ago through *Editions du Berger:*

This evening, June 6, 1990, I dropped by their house. I asked them, "Have you listened to the tapes? What do you think of them?"
—"Father, not only did I listen, but it cured me! I had been hospitalized with a spot on my lung. They all prayed to Mary and Jesus. Three days later no more spot. Here, this is the proof (his X-ray). I return your cassettes. I have copied them." Today both of them are Catholics. (Fr. F., to H., June 6, 1990).

I cite this case only by way of an example; these cures which cause joy and thanksgiving can be easily submitted to the official report.

The most staggering fruits are not seen: heroic conversions, a solution found for inextricable cases, through a total gift which assumes everything. Such an example is a couple, divorced and remarried, called to daily Eucharist and to the service of God. They have decided to live as brother and sister. A priest suggested to them to inquire if they could obtain an annulment of the first marriage of each in order to legalize the marriage of this perfectly harmonious couple. But they responded (fearing the laxity of clever canonists concerned with arranging everything):

—"We do not want to cheat either with God or with Our Lady."

On seeing their spiritual union and their apparent happiness, those who know their situation suspect them of duplicity. Why does one suspect evil so easily of Medjugorje? The knowledge of the realities indeed reveals spiritual marvels which discretion itself does not permit to reveal.

That does not prevent less commendable persons from making an incursion into this place of graces. In May 1990, a false priest made himself accepted and was given money in Medjugorje by a Swiss pilgrimage. It took a few days to unmask this clever crook. A phone call to Boston revealed that his name did not exist in the register of the archbishop. It is fatalistic that the attraction of Medjugorje also brings some black sheep and one watches there, as it was necessary to do in Lourdes in 1858, by inviting the pilgrims to prudence and discernment. These rare incidents should not become the trees that hide the forest. For each crook disguised as a priest, hundreds of priests find again a new spiritual breath, and vocations are born by the hundreds.

Msgr. Zanic performed a duty and made it a point to reveal the rare sins which could be committed more or less in relation to and with Medjugorje. He circulated 40,000 copies throughout the world of unfortunate incidents foreign to the pilgrimage. May he take into account the tremendous scale of edifying truths which the sense of decency, discretion and humility do not allow one to publish. It would result in a great balance for its discernment for the history of the event.

3. More Than Fifty Bishops at Medjugorje

For the last three or four years, bishops, distrustful because of the circulars of Msgr. Zanic, have become favorable toward Medjugorje, having seen the fruits which the pilgrims bring to their dioceses. It is for this reason that Cardinal Siri (one of the two *papabili* who obtained the most votes in the last two conclaves) confided to Bishop Hnilica, during a meeting in Genoa:

—"I have observed that people who have returned from Medjugorje return as apostles. They renew the parishes. They form prayer groups. They pray before the Blessed Sacrament. They lead other pilgrims to Medjugorje [. . .] and these prayer groups increase more and more. It is they who renew the Church. (Msgr. P. Hnilica, in *Sveta Bastina*, May 1990, reproduced in *Eco.*)

Thus a growing number of bishops have become pilgrims of Medjugorje. Their number is difficult to evaluate; many have gone there discreetly as formerly did Msgr. Franic in 1981. But more than 50 of them have been identified, and a good number have openly expressed themselves favorable.

Such is the case of Msgr. Donat Chiasson, age 60, Archbishop of Moncton (Canada), whose interview with Vicka has been reproduced in *L'Informateur* of Quebec:

> *Msgr. Chiasson:* Does Our Lady invite one especially to prayers of petition or of praise and adoration?
>
> *Vicka:* On several occasions the Blessed Virgin asked us to pray for the accomplishment of her intentions. As for prayer of praise or adoration, it is personal. That depends on each one. One has to experience it.
>
> *Msgr. Chiasson:* May we say that in our prayers we express our humility and our petitions, but the Eucharist is the greatest prayer of praise?
>
> *Vicka:* Yes, it is the prayer of praise, the greatest of all.

A journalist: Msgr. Chiasson, what is the reaction in your heart with respect to the phenomenon of Medjugorje?

Msgr. Chiasson: What delights me here is that the whole parish tries to live the Gospel without compromise. I do not have an opinion to express on the apparitions in Medjugorje. However, I believe in the message because it is consistent with the Gospel.

Numerous are the bishops who have come on a pilgrimage to Medjugorje in a private manner, with necessary discretion. The list is becoming longer. It undoubtedly is more than a hundred. Here are some names gathered at random from the circumstances.

In the spring of 1989:

—Msgr. P. Hnilica, Czechoslovakia

—Msgr. Federico Escaler, Bishop of the Prelacy of Ipil, suffragan from Zamboanga (Philippines)

—Msgr. Manuel Pinto Carvalheira, Bishop of Guarabira (Brazil)

—Another bishop from the vicinity of Rome came, remaining incognito (*Eco* 64, p. 3)

—Msgr. Homero Leit Imeria, Treca di Bahia (Brazil)

—Msgr. Deogratias S. Iniguez, Auxiliary Bishop of Malolos (Philippines)

—Msgr. Donald Raymond Lamont, Bishop Emeritus from Mutare (Zimbabwe)

—Three bishops incognito on June 25, 1989 (*Eco* 65)

—In the autumn of 1989, *Eco* gives the names of three other bishops from Indonesia, Philippines, and Haiti

The *Nouvelles de Medjugorje* give the following long list for this same autumn of 1989:

—Msgr. Patrick Flores, Archbishop of San Antonio

—Msgr. Edmond Cormodi, Auxiliary of the same diocese and two others. "I am here with the blessing of the Pope," said he.

—Msgr. Francesco Spenedda, Bishop of Oristano (Italy)

—Msgr. Gracian Mundadan, Syro-malabar Bishop of Bijnor (India)

—Msgr. G. Patrick Ziemann and Armando Ochoa, Auxiliary Bishops of Los Angeles

—Msgr. Franjo Komarica, Auxiliary of Banja Luka, president of the Commission of Inquiry who came *ex officio* for the first time

—Msgr. Anton Hoffman, Bishop Emeritus of Passau (West Germany)

—Msgr. Raymond Pezele, Bishop of Livingstone (Zambia)

—Msgr. Hilario Caves, Bishop of Nuevo Casas Grande (Mexico)

—Msgr. Mario Zanechini, Bishop Emeritus from Fidenza (Italy)

—Msgr. Generoso Camina Digos (Philippines)

—Msgr. Antonio Mabitas, Bishop from Davao and his Auxiliary Alfredo Baquial

—Msgr. Michael D. Pfeifer, Bishop of San Angelo, Texas, who presented at the Conference in Notre Dame (Indiana), a theology of Our Lady of Medjugorje: she is less a prophet of events to come than a help to discern more clearly the present.

—And indeed, others who requested to remain incognito, the bulletin *Nouvelles de Medjugorje,* December 1989, clearly states.

A new list was published by *Eco* in June 1990. Msgr. Francesco Spanedu, bishop on retreat, who came with a pilgrimage from Sardinia, was accompanied by Msgr. Franic. In his group was Giovanna Spanu, whose cure we report in the chronology.

The Msgr. Gabriel Diaz de Cueva (Ecuador), Msgr. Joseph Casale, Archbishop of Foggia, Italy, who stated:
—"Medjugorje is an extraordinary thing which invites us to change our lives. No one can remain indifferent about it. I will return." (*Eco,* no. 74.)

Msgr. Hnilica concluded his sermon on June 25, 1990, in Medjugorje:
—"Twenty million pilgrims, 22,000 priests, and about 100 bishops and cardinals without counting those who have come incognito. Certainly, they would have been noticed if anything did not go well [. . .]; if there were some danger for the faith, they would have intervened. Now then, they permit and they remain silent [. . .]. I say to the skeptics and to everyone: 'Come and see.' (*Eco,* no. 75.)

4. And the Pope?

John Paul II intends to stay above the debate and the investigations, which he follows opened to the spirit and with sympathy. But he remains faithful to the principle of subsidiary, honored by the Council: the higher echelon should intervene as little as possible in the competence of the lower echelon. He does not want to weigh over local activities. It is necessary then to respect his discretion and "not discover the crown," as the English say.

I will not then allow myself to narrate four conversations which I had with him on this subject, from a few seconds to some ten minutes. What he said to me, according to the same discretion, remains private. Many bishops have believed to be able, at their level, to confide his plans.

Msgr. Michael Pfeifer, bishop from Texas, writes in his pastoral letter of August 1987:

"In April of last year (1986) visit *ad limina*. With the bishops of Texas at the time of private conversation with the Holy Father, I asked him for his opinion on Medjugorje. The Pope answered in a very positive manner, and he called attention to everything good that the pilgrims could draw from it.

"At lunch, which the bishops of Texas had with the Pope, Medjugorje was again one of the topics of discussion. The Holy Father recognized that a large number of people changed their lives after their pilgrimage and the messages (in his knowledge) corresponded to the Gospel. A special commission always examines the events and, he stated clearly, there is not yet an official decision of the Church on the subject. John Paul II had observed the divergent warnings of the Yugoslav bishops on the phenomenon of Medjugorje." (*Stella Maris,* July-August 1989.)

Msgr. Mistorigo, Bishop of Triveneto (the Italian region where the positions are the most restrictive and negative on pilgrimages to Medjugorje), confided to *Vita del Popolo* (February 1987) his conversations with the Pope at the time of the five year visit *ad limina* of bishops from that region.
—"And did you speak about Medjugorje?" the journalist asked.

Msgr. Mistorigo: "We also spoke about that! The Pope indicated that he knew the situation well. At this place one prays; people approach the sacraments and they find there the occasion to promote a serious spiritual life. As regards a conclusion that there is a real presence of Mary, it is better to still remain prudent, because the evaluations of bishops and theologians are conflicting at this point."

Archbishop Patrick Flores (San Antonio, Texas), accompanied by two auxiliary bishops, reported his dialogue with John Paul II in January 1989:

1 and 2: Mirjana's apparition at Portland, Oregon (February 1990).
3: Marriage of Mirjana and Marco (September 18, 1989).
4: Mirjana at her 9th anniversary apparition (March 18, 1990).

5: Jelena and her father.

6: Apparition of Ivan and Maria (1990).

7: Fr. Jozo addresses the pilgrims (interpreter Cyrille Auboyneau).

8 and 9: Statue of Our Lady—St. Elijah Church—Tihaljina

10: Confessions at the church.
11: And the new confessionals.

12: The new outdoor altar.
13: Built behind the church.

14 and 15: New construction blends with the old.

16: A new village surrounding the church.
17: A new pilgrim's boarding house.

18: A new look in the valley.
19: Along with preservation of the old.

20 and 21: The continuous climb up Mt. Krizevac.

22: At dawn, at the Cross of Mt. Krizevac.
23: And on the Hill of Apparitions.

24: Ivan.
25: The new confessionals.

26: Prayer, shared at Mass.
27: Or during moments of solitude.

28: Fr. Jozo prays for pilgrims,
29: and for his brother priests.

16: As it is.
31: As it was.

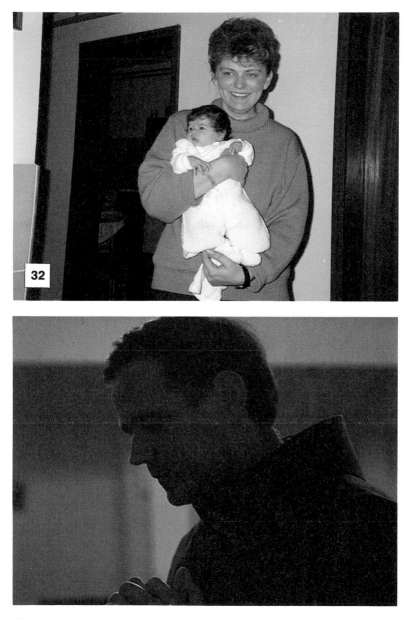

32: Mirjana and her daughter Maria.
Bottom photo: Fr. Jozo

Statue of Mary in St. James Church

I said to him, "Your Holiness, numerous persons from my diocese go to Medjugorje. I did not permit nor forbid them. What should I do?"

The Pope answered me, "Let the people go there. They pray there."

Encouraged by this response, I said to him, "But they are inviting me to accompany them in the month of August."

The Pope answerd, "Go, and pray for me."

It is thus that I find myself here in Medjugorje with the blessing of the Pope. (Remarks made in Medjugorje in August 1989, reported by *Message de paix,* Montreal, November-December 1989).

Msgr. Hnilica, a Czech bishop in exile, a friend of the Pope (already quoted in *Eight Years*), reported this remark by John Paul II, who was questioned on the opportunity of going on a pilgrimage to Medjugorje:
   —"If I were not the Pope, I would have been there
   a long time ago!"

Since then, Msgr. Hnilica has reported another remark by John Paul II, speaking to a group of doctors involved in the study of Medjugorje, on August 1, 1989:
   —"Yes, today the world has lost the sense of the
   supernatural. In Medjugorje, many have looked
   for it and found it in prayer, fasting, and
   confession."

   "These words of the Holy Father are the most
beautiful testimony on Medjugorje," concluded Msgr.
Hnilica (*Eco,* June 10, 1990).

In summary, the Pope does not express an opinion, does not interfere, but watches with sympathy and discreetly encourages those who go there, with the care to support the positive evolution of the matter. To another visitor who spoke to him about Medjugorje, he said:

"I pray every day for this intention."

Chapter 7

MESSAGES
(August, 1989-December, 1990)

August 21, 1989 at 10:30 p.m., to Ivan on Podbrdo, Hill of the Apparitions:

> *My children, this evening your mother calls you to live the messages which I give. Little children, I cannot give you other messages if you do not live the messages which I have already given. Decide with love, with joy, to begin to live my messages. Live my messages so that your mother may be able to guide you further and may be able to continue to help you in your growth.*

September 8, 1989 at 11:00 p.m., to Ivan on the Hill of the Apparitions:

> *My children, your mother asks you to pray as much as possible during these two days* (preparing for the Feast of the Holy Cross). *Abandon all your problems, all your difficulties to me. This evening I ask you, dear children, be joyful. Go in the peace of God.*

September 25, 1989, message to Maria for the parish:

> *Dear children, today I invite you to give thanks to God for all the gifts you have discovered in the course of your life, and even for the least gift you have perceived. I give thanks with you and want all of you to experience the joy of these gifts, and I want God to be everything for each one of you. And then, little children, you can grow continuously on the way of holiness. Thank you for having responded to my call.*

October 25, 1989, to Maria for the parish:

> *Dear children, today also I am inviting you to prayer. I am always inviting you, but you are still far away. Therefore, from today, decide seriously to dedicate time to God. I am with you and I wish to teach you to pray with the heart. In prayer with the heart you shall encounter God. Therefore, little children, pray, pray, pray! Thank you for having responded to my call.*

November 25, 1989.

> *Dear children, I am inviting you for years by these messages which I am giving you. Little children, by means of the messages I wish to make a very beautiful mosaic in your heart, so that I might be able to present each one of you to God like the original image. Therefore, little children, I desire that your decision be free before God, because He has given you freedom. Therefore, pray so that free from any influence of Satan, you may decide only for God. I am praying for you before God and I am seeking your surrender to God. Thank you for having responded to my call.*

December 25, 1989.

> *Dear children, today I am blessing you in a special way with my motherly blessing, and I am interceding for you before God that He will give you the gift of conversion of the heart. For years I am calling you and exhorting you to a deep spiritual life and simplicity. But you are so cold. Therefore, little children, I ask you to accept and to live the messages with seriousness so that your soul will not be sad when I will no longer be with you, and when I will no longer lead you like insecure children*

in their first steps. Therefore, little children, each day read the messages which I have given you and transform them into life. I love you and therefore, I am calling you all to the way of salvation with God. Thank you for having responded to my call.

December 25, 1989, to Ivan on Christmas night, on the hill of Podbrdo. (Mary was dressed in gold, surrounded by three angels. She had the baby Jesus in her arms. After having prayed, as usual, for those who were there, she said):

Dear children, here is my Son in my arms. I want to ask you to be the light for everyone. In this coming year, I invite you again to live my messages. They are messages of peace, prayer, conversion, penance, and faith. Dear children, your mother asks you not for words, but for acts. Your mother wants to help you and will give you the strength to continue. This evening I want to say to you: Rejoice!

The witnesses observed that the atmosphere of this nightly apparition was extraordinarily joyful.

1990

Monday, January 1, 1990, Feast of the Mother of God, message to Ivan on the hill of Podbrdo:

Your mother asks you, as she has already asked, to renew prayer in the family. Dear children, today the family is in need of prayer. Dear children, I wish that you would renew yourselves by living the messages through prayer in the family.

January 25, 1990, to Maria:

Dear children! Today I invite you to decide for God once again and to choose Him before everything and above everything, so that He may work miracles in your life and that day by day your life may become joy with Him. Therefore, little children, pray and do not permit Satan to work in your life through misunderstandings, not understanding and not accepting one another. Pray that you may be able to comprehend the greatness and the beauty of the gift of life. Thank you for having responded to my call.

February 2, 1990, message to Mirjana in the course of the apparition which took place in the chapel of the presbytery of the Church of St. Brigitte in Portland, Oregon. She received the following message:

I have been with you nine years. For nine years I wanted to tell you that God, your Father, is the only way, truth and life. I wish to show you the way to Eternal Life. I wish to be your tie, your connection to the profound faith. LISTEN TO ME!

Take your rosary and gather your children, your families with you. Give your good example to your children: give a good example to those who do not believe. You will not have happiness on this earth, neither will you come to Heaven if you are not with pure and humble hearts, and do not fulfill the law of God. I am asking for your help to join me to pray for those who do not believe. You are helping me very little. You have little charity or love for your neighbor and God gave you the love and showed you how you should forgive and love others. For that reason, reconcile and purify your soul. TAKE YOUR ROSARY AND PRAY IT. All your sufferings take patiently. You should remember that Jesus patiently suffered for you.

Let me be your Mother and your tie to God, to the Eternal Life. Do not impose your faith to unbelievers. Show it to them by your example and pray for them. MY CHILDREN, PRAY!

February 25, 1990, to Maria:

> *Dear children, I invite you to surrender to God. In this season I especially want you to renounce all the things to which you are attached, but are hurting your spiritual life. Therefore little children, decide completely for God and do not allow Satan to come into your life through those things that hurt both you and your spiritual life. Little children, God is offering Himself to you in fullness and you can discover and recognize Him only in prayer. Therefore, make a decision for prayer. Thank you for having responded to my call.*

March 25, 1990, to Maria:

> *Dear children, I am with you even if you are not conscious of it. I want to protect you from everything that Satan offers you and through which he wants to destroy you. As I bore Jesus in my womb, so also, dear children, do I wish to bear you unto holiness. God wants to save you and sends you messages through man, nature, and so many things which can only help you to understand that you must change the direction of your life. Therefore, little children, understand also the greatness of the gift which God is giving you through me, so that I may protect you with my mantle and lead you to the joy of life. Thank you for having responded to my call.*

April 13, 1990, Good Friday, to Ivan on the hill of Krizevac at 11:30 p.m.:

> *Dear children, I am very happy to see you this evening. Know, dear children, that at the foot of the Cross, when my Son died, I was alone with some women. I am happy to see you together here so numerous. This evening, on returning to your homes, pray the Rosary and give thanks to God.*

That evening, after having prayed and extended her hands over those who surrounded Ivan at night, she continued to pray in an exceptional way, but without Ivan hearing her voice.

April 16, 1990, Monday of Easter Week, on the hill of Podbrdo, to Ivan at 11:30 p.m. The Blessed Virgin, having appeared with the three angels, illuminating with a pascal joy, only asked that one pray for her intentions. She prayed with those in attendance, and while praying, she went away in the sign of the luminous cross while saying: *Go in peace, dear children.*

April 25, 1990.

> *Dear children! Today I invite you to accept with seriousness and to live the messages which I am giving you. I am with you and I desire, dear children, that each one of you be ever closer to my heart. Therefore, little children, pray and seek the will of God in your everyday life. I desire that each one of you discover the way of holiness and grow in it until eternity. I will pray for you and intercede for you before God that you understand the greatness of this gift which God is giving me that I can be with you. Thank you for having responded to my call.*

May 25, 1990, to Maria:

> *Dear children, I invite you to decide with seriousness to live this novena. Consecrate the time to prayer and to sacrifice. I am with you, and I desire to help you to grow in renunciation and mortification that you may be able to understand the beauty of the life of people who go on giving themselves to me in a special way. Dear children, God blesses you day after day and desires a change of your life. Therefore pray that you may have the strength to*

change your life. Thank you for having responded to my call.

June 25, 1990.

Dear children, today I desire to thank you for all your sacrifices and for all your prayers. I am blessing you with my special motherly blessing. I invite you all to decide for God, so that from day to day you will discover His will in prayer. I desire, dear children, to call all of you to a full conversion so that joy will be in your hearts. I am happy that you are here today in such great numbers. Thank you for having responded to my call.

July 25, 1990, to Maria:

Today I invite you to peace. I have come here as the Queen of Peace, and I desire to enrich you with my motherly peace. Dear children, I love you, and I wish to bring all of you to the peace which only God gives and which enriches every heart. I invite you to become carriers and witnesses of my peace in this unpeaceful world. Let peace reign in the whole world, which is without peace and which longs for peace. I bless you with my motherly love.

August 6, 1990, apparition to Ivan on the hill of Podbrdo: The Blessed Virgin invites all to recite the Glorious Mysteries before the cross.

August 25, 1990, to Maria:

Today I invite you to take seriously and put into practice the messages which I am giving you. You know, little children, that I am with you, that I desire to lead you along the same path to Heaven which is beautiful for those who discover it in prayer.

Therefore, little children, do not forget that these messages which I am giving you have to be put into your everyday life in order that you might be able to say: "There, I have taken the messages and I am trying to live them." Dear children, I am protecting you before the Heavenly Father by my own prayers.

September 25, 1990.

Dear children, I invite you to pray with the heart in order that your prayer may be a conversation with God. I desire each one of you to dedicate more time to God. Satan is strong and wants to destroy and deceive you in many ways. Therefore, dear children, pray every day that your life will be good for yourself and for all those you meet.

I am with you, and I am protecting you even though Satan wishes to destroy my plans and to hinder the desires which the heavenly Father wants to realize here. Thank you for having responded to my call.

October 25, 1990, to Maria, the monthly message:

Dear children. Today I call you to pray in a special way and to offer up sacrifices and good deeds for peace in the world. Satan is strong and with all his strength tries to destroy the peace which comes from God. Therefore, dear children, pray in a special way with me for peace. I am with you and I desire to help you with my prayers, and I desire to guide you on the path of peace. I bless you with my motherly blessing. Do not forget to live the messages of peace. Thank you for having responded to my call.

November 25, 1990, to Maria, for the parish:

Dear children, today I invite you to do works of mercy with love and out of love for me and for your brothers and sisters. All that you do for others, do it with great joy and humility toward God. I am with you, and day after day I offer your sacrifices and prayers to God for the salvation of the world. Thank you for having responded to my call.

December 25, 1990, to Maria, for the parish:

Dear children, today I invite you in a special way to pray for peace. Dear children, without peace you cannot experience the birth of the Child Jesus, neither today nor in your daily lives. Therefore, pray to the Lord of Peace that He may protect you with His mantle and that He may help you to comprehend the greatness and importance of peace in your hearts. In this way, you shall be able to spread peace from your hearts throughout the whole world.

I am with you and intercede for you before God. Pray, because Satan wants to destroy my plan of peace. Be reconciled with one another, and by means of your lives, work that peace may reign in the whole earth. Thank you for having responded to my call.

Chapter 8

WHERE IS MEDJUGORJE GOING?

Apocalypse?

What about the secrets of Medjugorje? One can say almost nothing about them: content, credibility, date of disclosure. They are secrets. The visionaries have pointed out only their meaning and purpose.

Certain indications seemed to announce their accomplishment as imminent in 1984; the year when the reign of Satan was going to come to an end as the letter of Tomislav Vlasic to the Pope suggests (December 1983). Mirjana, who stopped having apparitions at Christmas 1982, again had occasional apparitions and locutions to establish the plan for this revelation. But six years later, we are at the same point.

Yet, several visionaries (not all) say that they know the date. I had thought for a moment that they knew only the day and the month, not the year. But Mirjana and Vicka told me precisely that they knew also the year. Under these conditions, one misunderstands Mirjana's haste in 1984 to prepare the mechanism for the revelation of the secrets. There is mystery and a lot of questions without answers.

Let us not be surprised about it. Every apocalypse, every prediction of the future has its part of uncertainty and of ambiguity. It projects flashing but fleeting lights about a future, which the prophet himself does not understand.

The apocalyptical is no less respectable; it has its place in the Bible: With Ezekiel, Isaiah 24-27, Joel 3-4, Zachariah 9-14, finally and especially the apocalyptic discourse of Christ (Matthew 24 and similar ones, over which exegetes still labor today), and the Apocalypse of St. John which ends the Bible.

What is the apocalypse? The disclosure of hidden mysteries concerning more particularly the human and cosmic future, the accomplishment of the history of salvation—the "day of the Lord," the coming of God, the return of Christ.

All that is not in vain. Everything has a basis. But it is a fact that this literature remains ambiguous, obscure, its

110

interpretations discussed. It has flourished more in the apocryphal books than in the Bible. If these values and this hope have a place, it is not a central place. They must remain alive, but it is dangerous for them to proliferate by intruding into the field of the Christian conscience, called more profoundly to live in union with God. This union with God (with His power as with His love), is a more secure pledge of the future which cannot deceive. It is radical and more important than the apocalyptic and prophetic glimpses toward a future uncertain to human eyes, for "the Son Himself does not know either the day or the hour," said Jesus (*Mk.* 13:32).

Is the Apocalyptic a temptation? No, if it vivifies the dynamic hope of the return of God, His daily return, His ultimate return; yes, if it forgets that this coming of God is carried out each day, discreetly, profoundly, intimately in each life and prepares a sure future which surpasses and escapes us. Far from being the essential or the more important, the ten secrets received in Medjugorje are a secondary aspect, indeed marginal, not the main focus.

The Three Days of Darkness

For two years I have been asked twenty times, especially in the United States, on the prophesy of the "three days of darkness" which threatens the world, and the rumor has circulated that the Blessed Virgin had spoken about it in Medjugorje. According to some printed material, largely distributed by *Michael Journal* (Rougemont, Quebec Province, Canada, January-February 1990), Fr. David Lopez, an American religious from the Hermitage of Ternora (Texas), is supposed to have had the following locution on August 15, 1987, in Medjugorje.

> "During the three days of darkness, there will no longer be devils in Hell. They will all be on earth. These three days will be so dark that we will not even be able to see our own hands [. . .]. Close your windows and blinds and do not listen to anyone who will call you from the outside [. . .]. Tell

the people not to look at signs and not to lose their
time looking for the exact days when these events
will take place [. . .].

"The days of darkness will last exactly 72 hours.
You will be able only to foresee the end if you have
a spring watch, for there will be no more electricity."

Of course, these somber predictions, attributed to David
Lopez, are preceded and intermingled with judicious invitations not to fear, for there is no fear for him who is in the
hands of God. Let us consider the fact. The pious prophet
invites one to a repentance, an urgency in charity. And the
temporal limits of the trial (three days) are of a nature in
order to avoid panic, for after this darkness and this corrup-
tion of the elements:

"everything will become light and green again and
the water will be like crystal: there will no longer
be contamination of the rivers and of the water. And
the most beautiful thing will be the new life of the
people."

With all due respect to Fr. Lopez, one cannot find these
three days of darkness anywhere in the messages of Medjugorje. Maria, whom I consulted over the matter, firmly excluded it. Likwise Ivan, to whom people attributed such
remarks.

The message of Medjugorje can be summarized in this: conversion, return to God, faith, prayer, fasting, and through this
way, reconciliation and peace. That is what is essential, solid,
and guaranteed by the Gospel. Our Lady reminds us of its
urgency in our suicidal world. Such is the tenor of the first
messages and the pedagogical clarifications disseminated since
then for nine years.

As for the three days of darkness, they call for many reservations for the following reasons:

1. The Bible and Christian tradition invite us not to yield to the vertigo of the prophets of calamity. To focus one's attention on the negative is, whether one likes it or not, to sink into it. For whatever the essential place of the Cross in the work of redemption may be, the message of Christ above all invites us to faith, joy, optimism, hope.

2. The polarization of the prophesies of calamity often causes one to squander, uselessly, many means of living which could have been better used. In these last years, how many people (because of this prophesy or others similar) have stock-piled food and water, or expensive items in a self-styled protected fortress (in France, Brittany) in order to enter the shelter from uncertain predictions announced. That does not actualize their life, or the credibility of Christianity.

3. The success of this prophecy results from its rich poetic tenor. The "three days of darkness" is certainly a beautiful formula. It is inspired in the Bible. It recalls the three days of the death of Christ and the darkness which began with his death. It is tempting to project these three days to the end of the world, and this end of the world, in a near future. A formula, so well struck, makes it own way. It easily returns through association of ideas or images, including from the lips of true visionaries. One must be careful.

4. The prediction of the three days of darkness has been told well before Medjugorje. Anne-Marie Taigi (1769-1837) already said:
—"There will come over the earth immense darkness lasting three days and three nights."
—When? No one has stated it precisely for two centuries. Many others have repeated it since then in moving and diverse ways. I do not see that one can draw from that with any precision on the future.

Let us found and balance our lives on God Himself and His inspiration, as the message of Medjugorje invites us. Let us not project so quickly to the future that which belongs only to God, a mixture of authentic inspirations and fantasies which no one is in the process of unraveling. Those who have at times authentically and precisely predicted the future did not understand it before it materialized. (R. Laurentin, *Predictions de Mere Yvonne-Aimee de Malestroit,* Paris, O.E.I.L., 1987).

The future belongs to God, but also to us. And we have to live it with God, not by buying spring watches in anticipation of the three days of darkness, but by developing our life of prayer, fasting, the gift of ourselves, of service, and of charity in living the message of the Gospel and Our Lady. We have seen that in this manner, conversions, vocations, prayer groups, new religious families, and spiritual or social initiatives of all kinds are born.

Awakening in the Youth

Among the youth of today, so abandoned, so often misguided, the message given to the young visionaries in Medjugorje has brought about the rise of a new generation of young Christians on an international scale. The visionaries are young, full of life, sympathetic, dynamic, radiating with joy, courage and holiness. Their testimony convinces and influences, including young people who recognize their future in this model. From there comes a harvest of vocations which rises in Medjugorje and elsewhere in closed ranks.

This springtime of youth the Blessed Virgin had stimulated by calling together a "Year of the Youth," August 15, 1988-August 15, 1989. Thousands of them came to bring it to a close in Medjugorje through fasting, prayer, in preparation for August 15, 1989. The movement did not end. According to a new message, the young people were invited to return to Medjugorje from July 30 to August 6, 1990. There were more than 5,000. They will repeat this "festival of prayer" next year.

This springtime of youth and of vocations is only a trickle within the immense current of spiritual renewal, which is awakening everywhere and seems to announce new times for the Church and for the world.

The youth, very often surrendered to the most basic instincts because of a lack of education, is capable of an immense generosity. A treasure of potentialities dwells in the rising generations. They are the future. Medjugorje shows it. Its fruits are alredy substantial. Our Lady, who has come to help a world in danger, has a particular concern for the youth. In San Nicolás (Argentina), as in Medjugorje, her messages cause an authentic renewal.

That agrees with the invitation of John Paul II: "We are on the threshold of a new millennium and a new world." This world, sure of itself (for a long time sure of its atheism in the East), has cracked. Persecutions are in recession. Freedoms are reborn. One can ask himself whether the conversion of Russia, announced in Fatima, then in Medjugorje, is not in progress now. It is the news today that God is in the Russian media, and the parishes do not suffice for the demands for baptism which are by the hundreds in many parishes. And John Paul II invites us to make the last ten years of our century a long Advent with Mary, who has an important role to play for a new birth of Christ in this world.

In Medjugorje, one indeed recognizes the Blessed Virgin of the Gospel, Mother of the Lord and Mother of mankind, concerned over her children. She presents herself under the signs of the *Apocalypse* 12:1-20, as in Guadalupe and the Rue du Bac. She is the woman "Clothed With the Sun" (the light of Christ precedes her, transfigures her, and disappears at her departure). She is crowned with 12 stars. She inspires the love of Christ, prayer, generosity, the gift of self, courage in tribulations of which she set an example on Calvary. She ardently invites us to do everything the Lord tells us (*Jn.* 2:5). These values are the future of Medjugorje. God will do the rest.

Prayer of the Heart

The essential axis of Medjugorje is the Gospel message of conversion, prayer, peace. The most frequent theme, the most insistent in this message, is prayer. Our Lady does not tire of repeating: pray, pray, pray! The beautiful point of this message is the invitation to prayer of the heart. The visionaries practice it and teach it.

What is it about? A profound operation: a conversation of the heart in order to involve the whole being—spirit, heart, and body in love with God alone, through the hands of Mary our mother.

What is the heart? It is not only the physical organ, the muscle of circulation of the blood. It is more. "The heart" shows (in the Bible), this vital point of our free conscience, whence come the impulses, the choices, the profound and motivated decisions.

The whole Bible is summarized in one doctrine of Christian experience—an experience of the spirit and experience of the heart. For the Bible does not separate the Holy Spirit, source of all creation and all inspiration, and the human "heart" which receives these inspirations at the key point of our entire being. From the first page of the Bible, the Spirit is there, over the waters of creation (*Gen.* 1:1). Then God breathes the spirit into man, pinnacle of His creation. Man is formed from the earth; God puts in him a spark of divine fire. The Spirit speaks to the heart of man to make him pass from a conventional faith to a living faith. For, to believe is undoubtedly to adhere to invisible truths revealed by God; it is to obey them, for revelation is also a commandment.

But the prophets of Israel, pioneers of the New Testament, and Christ Himself taught us to pass from an exterior faith to an interior faith, from a mental knowledge to a gift, and interior adherence of love. The prophet Jeremiah revealed a decisive stage in announcing the interiorization of the law. It had been given to Moses on tables of stone, from the exterior, and God announced to Jeremiah (31:33-34):

> —*This is the alliance which I will conclude with the house of Israel in those days—Oracle of Yahweh—I will place My law within them, and I will write it on their heart. I will be their God and they will be my people. And no one will have*

to teach his neighbor, no one his brother in saying: "Know Yahweh," for all of them will know
me from the least to the greatest: Oracle of
Yahweh.

After him, Ezekiel (36:25-27) reveals more before the
promise:
—*I will purify you* [. . .] *and I will give you a new
heart, and I will put a new spirit in you.*

What he describes is not only the inscription of the law
in the human heart, it is an astonishing surgical operation
(spiritual, for sure):
—*I will take away from your flesh the heart of stone,
and I will give you a heart of flesh.* (*Ezekiel* 36:26).

It is no longer the circumcision of the heart of which Jeremiah
spoke (4:4 and 9:24-26). It is a more radical novelty: the
transfer, the heart implantation by God in man in a human
degree. It is the interior graft of a new spiritual organ of grace,
a new freedom, sensitive to God, animated by a new spirit.
It is in this new heart that the Holy Spirit will be able to enter.
—*I will put my spirit within you and make you live
by my statutes, careful to observe my decrees.*
(*Ezekiel* 36:27).

The new heart, animated by the new spirit, is the new life
of the new creation—that which since then, from generation
to generation even in the worst periods, seized on Christians
who were dull (such as the easy and golden youth of the rich,
bourgeois Francis of Assisi), and caused it to be born to a
new life, animated by new gifts: the charisms foreseen by
Joel 3:1-3:
—*I will pour out My Spirit over all flesh. Your sons
and your daughters will prophesy. Your old people
will have dreams and your young people visions,*
etc.

It is the realization of this collection of prophecies that the
Apostle Peter welcomes on the day of Pentecost (*Acts* 2:17-19).
We are heirs to these promises, but we do not live them.

Our heart, the new heart received in baptism, is often as if dead, lethargic. And we remain at a verbal, external prayer. The Blessed Virgin invites us to take up life again, to re-animate the new heart which has been given us: a heart in tune with the rhythm of God, to its wave length, capable of capturing the breath of the spirit. This is "prayer of the heart."

It was necessary to evoke these realities, which are unrecognized today. "He who can understand, let him understand!"

It is a matter of believing them, of no longer shutting our faith within a closed intellectuality, at times well structured but dead like the bones of Ezekiel, for it remains eternal to God, His revelation, His love. It is a matter of waking up our heart, including the heart of the flesh which dwells in our breast, and to make the prayer of our minds descend there so that our entire being is involved in prayer, even to our guts. This transfer, this physical expansion of prayer into our whole being, will help the awakening of the spiritual heart which God has given us. The words of the prayer will become spirit and flame (prayer of the heart), according to a frequent experience in Medjugorje. The problems will become spirit.

This was the grace of Mary. She was the first to receive a total, preventive purification and the new creation of the heart. In this way, she was able to take up in God the immense and fruitful joys and sufferings of life. Thus, she became Mother of God and of us, with a multiple heart.

Chapter 9

APPENDICES

INTERVIEWS OF THE VISIONARIES AND OTHERS

At the request of readers, we continue to give, in an appendix, some excerpts of the main interviews of the visionaries which have been published throughout the world.

INTERVIEW OF JELENA VASILJ
(August 5, 1987)

Question: Speak to us about fasting.
Jelena: The Gospa says that fasting helps us to grow in Christian life; not only fasting on bread and water but also fasting from so many things that we like. She says to do it always with the heart, like a pleasure, and not out of duty.

Question: For the Gospa, what do "mortification" and "penance" mean?
Jelena: An attentive awakening on the way.

Question: Sometimes we pray, but our thoughts are elsewhere.
Jelena: One must put himself in the hands of the Lord because we cannot change our heart; we have to pray so that He may help us. (Reported by Alberto Bonifacio, published in *Eco.*)

INTERVIEW OF VICKA BY S. FERRARO
(Beginning February, 1989)

S. Ferraro: This publicity which has made you climb to number one in the journals, has it not changed you?

Vicka: What has happened to us, to us six, is a truly marvelous thing, but it is a great gift from the Lord, and a gift destined for all mankind. It is for the salvation of the human race that the Gospa appears to us and communicates her messages to us each day.

S. Ferraro: How does she appear?

Vicka: She is very beautiful; her beauty is indescribable! She does not resemble any woman that I know. She wears a long gray robe and a white veil. She appears to me as a person of flesh and bones; it is not an abstract vision. When it is time, she is there before me and we speak to each other.

S. Ferraro: At what time do you see her?

Vicka: She arrives at 5:40 every afternoon. The vision lasts about five minutes and sometimes a little longer.

S. Ferraro: What does the Gospa tell you?

Vicka: She communicates to me messages for mankind...for the salvation of the human race.

S. Ferraro: What messages?

Vicka: They are messages of prayer, faith, conversion, fasting, penance, and of peace [. . .]. We are the mouthpieces for the salvation of all. My role is to be a witness to the words of the Gospa and to receive the pilgrims who come to my home. It is the vocation of my life.

S. Ferraro: Did you believe in God before the Gospa appeared?

Vicka: Yes, I was a believer and practicing in an ordinary way, as young people at the age of 16 to 18 can be with so many problems and so many illusions. Then the Gospa came and my life changed completely. I do not really know why she chose me.

S. Ferraro: And those famous secrets which the Gospa revealed to you, what can you say?

Vicka: Of course, I cannot say anything precisely. These secrets are of vital importance for mankind. They concern the destiny of the world. But the mother of God has forbidden us to reveal them before time. Two of my friends, Mirjana and Ivanka, already know all ten secrets and no longer see the Gospa everyday as we, but only once a year [. . .].

S. Ferraro: Have you lived any supernatural experiences during this period?

Vicka: If it is a matter of miracles and strange powers, no. To tell the truth, following the apparitions, there have been recorded many inexplicable cures and signs in the heavens which have been given to us, but nothing else. The Gospa has explained to us that these happenings are only designed to help the most skeptical. Yet, a marvelous thing personally happened to me. Some years ago [in fact on Thursday, November 12, 1981] I was with Jakov, and the Blessed Virgin appeared to us. She took us by the hand and we visited paradise, purgatory, and Hell. It was not a dream, for we really disappeared for 20 minutes as Jakov's mother confirmed. In paradise there was a great light which does not exist on the earth, and many happy people, all dressed alike; in purgatory, a great cloud, impenetrable, in which one heard lamentations, moanings of suffering. Finally, in Hell, a great fire and some persons hurled themselves willingly into it and were transformed into ugly animals which blasphemed.

INTERVIEW WITH MIRJANA DRAGICEVIC
(Medjugorje, March 26, 1989, Easter Sunday)

The interview was recorded by Maria Rosa Pirelli and Dom Pietro Zorza.

D. Zorza: Many of us have come to Medjugorje for the first time. Can you tell us what is the most important thing in Medjugorje?

Mirjana: For me it is to pray for the unbelievers. The Gospa repeats that she is in need of our prayers, our help for them. She is like a mother concerned for everyone. She recalls the secrets which she has given and her concern is for unbelievers, for they do not know what is awaiting them. [...] She has told me that. She told Ivan that one must pray more for young people; to Ivanka, for the souls in purgatory.

D. Zorza: Can you give us a synthesis of the messages since the beginning of the apparitions?

Mirjana: She tells us that we have forgotten everything that is written in the Bible: to pray for our deceased, have Mass celebrated for them. [...] Even if our dead are in paradise, we can have Mass celebrated. [...] She also says not to turn away from the old and the poor because they are in need of our help. For Mass, she says: in church it is necessary to feel like in our home where our parents are, where one can always go and say what one wishes. She says to go more often to church. The Gospa says that the Rosary is very important and that it is necessary to pray always, for through it we can obtain all that we want.

D. Zorza: We read that when the daily apparitions ended for you at Christmas 1982, you had great difficulty. Why?

Mirjana: Because when you see a very beautiful thing, more beautiful than everything, and then suddenly you no longer see it...

D. Zorza: Father Jozo [the parish priest at the time of the first apparitions] told us that he has also seen the Gospa.

Mirjana: I know. Once, while we were praying the Rosary, we had already begun to see the Madonna on the altar. He began to pray the Hail Mary, he stopped. Everyone in church had observed that everything was not as usual. He began to pray with greater force. Through it, I had understood that he also had seen the Gospa.

D. Zorza: Can you describe for us the Madonna in her beauty?

Mirjana: It is not possible because on earth there is nothing of similar beauty. It is not only beauty, it is also light. And then it is her countenance. One sees that she is from another life: not with our concerns, but a peace.

D. Zorza: Even when there are problems throughout the world?

Mirjana: Yes.

D. Zorza: Have you seen her sad sometimes?

Mirjana: Yes, often, when she speaks of unbelievers. By unbelievers, the Madonna also includes the people who go to church but who do not have their hearts open to God, not living the faith in their souls.

D. Zorza: What do you, the visionaries, do in order to be so filled with joy? Even you, now?

Mirjana: Today is Easter Sunday!

D. Zorza: But other times also I have seen you filled with joy, even though you know the ten secrets and what is going to fall on the world. What gives you the strength to be so filled with joy?

Mirjana: The credit goes to the Gospa, for without her help we cannot be normal. Of that I am sure.

D. Zorza: The last two secrets [we read it in the interview which you gave Fr. Tomislav] are irreversible and must come even if the world is converted.[1]

Mirjana: It is not possible for the secrets to change even if the world is converted.

D. Zorza: Then will the last two secrets come to pass also?

Mirjana: All of them!

D. Zorza: But if all of us are converted and become saints and the whole world becomes a saint, will the ten secrets come to pass?

Mirjana: Listen, it is not possible for the whole world to become a saint; even when Jesus came to earth many did not believe in Him. It is so now. . .of that I am sure. [. . .]

D. Zorza: And yet you prayed very much and the seventh secret was softened.

Mirjana: But after that, Our Lady told me that it was not possible to change again. With respect to the rest, the seventh secret was not changed. It was only reduced a little.

D. Zorza: Ivanka told me that she knew how the world will be after the ten secrets.

Mirjana: We do not speak among ourselves about the secrets. We only know that I received ten secrets and that Ivanka received ten secrets. Perhaps they are not the same. That is why we do not speak about them.

D. Zorza: Do you not say anything among yourselves?

Mirjana: Among ourselves, we do not speak about the apparitions.

D. Zorza: Tell us about your last apparition.

Mirjana: The Gospa spoke to me about unbelievers; she was sad and wants our prayers. She spoke to me also about the secrets. [. . .]

D. Zorza: Explain to us, to us priests also, what to do in order to become saints?

Mirjana: The Gospa does not ask for much; she only wants for the heart to be open to God. You have to feel Him like your father, go to church with love, and not because it is necessary to go there. [. . .]

D. Zorza: What you have said is very beautiful: to experience God as your father. How do you experience Him?

Mirjana: When I went to catechism, I always saw God as a man with a beard, Who looked at my sins to grumble at me. I think that it is wrong for priests (pardon me) to say: God watches you and then grumbles at you. But no priest told me: "Experience God like your father, go to church and tell Him what you want, what hurts you, open your heart to God." I had great fear of God because I did not think that He was good. It seemed to me that He grumbled without love.

D. Zorza: How do you experience Him now?

Mirjana: Normally, as my Father who wishes me well, but

Who grumbles at me also when I make a choice that is not good.

D. Zorza: Do you experience Him really like your Father?

Mirjana: Yes, absolutely. I so experience His love when I pray with my heart. When one wants something with an open heart, it is sure that He will help us, and I have indeed seen how He has helped me so many times!

D. Zorza: Give an example.

Mirjana: Everything that I have asked for has come. Yes, everything, thanks to God! [. . .] I prayed for two years to find a job because I wanted to work, and so one day I found the job (at the tourist agency in Medjugorje). [. . .]

D. Zorza: And Jesus, how do you experience Him?

Mirjana: Like a brother.

D. Zorza: Like a brother, really?

Mirjana: I was studying and I still had two exams before my schooling would be finished. When I do poorly on an exam, I go immediately to church [. . .]; it is normal becaue we are a family. We have a father, a mother, and a brother who want very much the best for us. [. . .]

D. Zorza: In the interview of Fr. Tomislav, you wanted to know so many things, you were curious and you wanted to present so many questions to the Gospa! Has the Gospa always answered you?

Mirjana: Yes, when they are requests for her; when it is not for her, I do not even ask. I was lucky to be alone in Sarajevo; I was able to speak to her about everything. The other visionaries [in Medjugorje] did not have the possibility because they received all kinds of requests. I was alone and able to speak of so many other things. [. . .]

D. Zorza: For example?

Mirjana: I do not succeed in recalling a specific example. . .everything that interests me in life.

FOOTNOTE

1. It is Mirjana's belief. Others, such as Maria, stress that prayer and fasting can change anything.

INTERVIEW OF MARIA PAVLOVIC
(Medjugorje, April 15, 1989)

Question: Maria, you have just lived some important moments. What can you tell us about them?

Maria: The Gospa appeared to me every day in America (November 1988-January 1989). During the first days after the operation, her visits lasted shorter than usual. The Blessed Virgin always gave me her blessing and that was for me the occasion of a deep evolution, bound to the offering which I made to God on behalf of my brother [her kidney was donated to him]. For my part, this process represented really an intense joy and a great enrichment: not only what I gave, but also what I received, and I obtained very special graces throughout this time [. . .]. My greatest happiness was the presence of the Queen of Peace at my side during the two hour operation. She said nothing, but the expression on her face changed constantly. Her visit obtained for me a living joy, especially after the oblation, at the moment when the sufferings intensified.

Question: Explain more this apparition under anesthesia.

Maria: She had informed me the day before that she would be near me, but I did not know what she meant by that. I had talked with the doctors and I had informed them that I would perhaps have an apparition, in case they would report an extraordinary phenomenon. Her visit was prolonged during two hours. The surgeon declared that God alone had been able to direct the course of the intervention.

Question: Did you see yourself and the course of the operation?

Maria: I did not see anything of the intervention. I only saw the Mother of God.

Question: Before you?

Maria: No, she remained above me. The expression on her face changed constantly. At the beginning, she was serious. Then her expression became joyful. When everything was over, I guessed from her attitude.

Question: How long did the operation last?

Maria: According to what they told me, three and a half hours.

Question: You saw her for two hours. Did you fall asleep again when she disappeared?

Maria: Indeed I do not know exactly if it was two hours. Nevertheless, I distinguished perfectly when the Gospa arrived, then when she left, but after the time of her departure, I do not remember anything.

Question: How did you reach a decision to give a kidney to your brother?

Maria: If was, of course, my love for Andrija which prevailed at that time. Every time that I asked myself this question, my family was against my intention. That even raised problems at the presbytery. It was a very difficult situation for me. I saw my responsibility, but they kept reminding me that my health was not very strong. I maintained that I would submit myself to a preparatory medical exam in America. If such was the will of God, I would donate a kidney and everything would go well. If the doctors determined that I was not able to give this organ to my brother, I was ready to accept that decision. I left in this frame of mind. I thought that perhaps complications would arise. Yet, everything developed in the best conditions. That was for me the sign that the gift of my kidney to Andrija corresponded well to the Divine Will.

Question: How important is it to you that Our Lady discloses messages for the parish and the world?

Maria: What the mother of God wants proves very important for me. It is a way.

Question: How are your days going, currently [April 1989]?

Maria: On the advice of the doctors, I decided not to receive any pilgrims in groups for a period of time. But there are always some good friends here [. . .]. At this time I can devote myself more specially to isolated persons. Previously, I spent much time with groups [. . .]. Presently, I have to care for myself. Nevertheless, I accomplish my usual tasks as previously.

Question: How much time do you find for prayer?

Maria: Since before my return to Medjugorje, I had decided to reserve more time for prayer, to be more assiduous to prayer. Now I dispose of sufficient time and I have an excuse to justify my isolation. There are very different opinions on prayer. Some people consider equally work and prayer. Nevertheless, I feel very strongly that in more of what I do, I have to arrange some time for prayer. That is easier for me at this time, thanks to my illness.

Question: What environment is there for the group of visionaries?

Maria: We meet each Thursday; it is a great joy that we share among ourselves. The parish priest [Fr. Leonard Orec] has helped us very much from this point of view. We simply see how each are developing: for example, Ivanka as a mother. We have embraced her even more. We perceive her as a mother [of little Kristina].

Question: Our Lady has asked us to pray constantly. What is your experience on this matter?

Maria: According to the Gospa, the essential thing is that we think always of God. She stated specifically that our work can likewise become prayer. We must, of course, determine the time that we can devote to prayer alone, but at the same time, it is necessary for us to decide to transform our entire day into prayer. With the help of short prayers, we can always give thanks to God and unite ourselves permanently with Him in our thoughts. We attain it in different ways. We know that the saints remained in prayer for hours. The Gospa invites us on the road to holiness. It represents a main exhortation addressed to each one of us. We are all called to opt for the way of holiness.

Question: You once said to me that the whole day passed in waiting for the meeting with Mary.

Maria: Of course, for us each day is a new meeting day. To be in the presence of the Queen of Peace represents an extreme happiness which I cannot express. That moment is the most important of our entire life. There is absolutely nothing else which can take on such a value, because our heavenly mother knows us. She knows everything that concerns us, and she meets us with love; she loves us. It is impossible to compare her to any other human being.

(*Stella Maris,* December 1989)

INTERVIEW OF VICKA IVANKOVIC
(Spring 1989)

Question: Vicka, on September 25, 1988, Our Lady ended your suffering which lasted several years. Can you tell us the circumstances?

Vicka: The Gospa had told me several months previously that my illness would cease. But I did not disseminate it because it was a certainty for me alone. Two members of the commission came here when the cure approached. They asked me: "Vicka, would you be able to put in writing for us when it will take place so that we will open this letter later and can verify the exactness?" I answered: "Yes!" They were here in this room. They took two envelopes: one for me and one for them. I wrote the date, put it in the envelope which I sealed.

Two or three days before September 25, I informed them that they should come. The president in charge of the Commission of Inquiry by the Yugoslav Episcopal Conference [auxiliary bishop of Banja Luka] arrived in the company of three other priests. It was together that we opened the envelope.

Question: Could you give some concrete information related to your suffering? Because people have written a lot on this subject: some true and some false. . .

Vicka: I suffered some violent migraines during almost three and a half years. Actually, I was never really concerned with the origin of these headaches. I always said interiorly: "Thank You, my God! You know why I endure these sufferings. I am wholly at Your disposal." It is important for man to receive trials with the approval of his heart. If the Gospa has imposed a cross or an illness on me (whatever it was), it was always essential that I accept it with love. I never asked: "My God, why?" I constantly repeated that if there were still something else, He could quietly give it to me because I wished to take it also.

Question: Yet it must have harmed you very much. It affected you so that you were unable to get up.

Vicka: I was confined to my bed at times but rarely. Perhaps one, two, or three hours. When I had these migraines,

I did not suffer everywhere, but only here [she shows the exact place of the pain]. I went to Zagreb for a physical exam, but they found nothing [. . .].

Question: What is our heavenly mother currently talking to you about?

Vicka: She recommends us to pray, above all for the young people who actually find themselves in a very difficult situation. We can only and simply help them by our friendship and our prayer of the heart. The Gospa states: "Dear children, this period is a time of great graces. I wish that you begin to live the messages with the heart." She wishes for us to become the heralds of her peace and for us to pray for harmony in the world [. . .].

Question: How many times will she still come?

Vicka: She has not said anything about it at the present time.

Question: Has she recently recalled catastrophes?

Vicka: No. She states that we must not live in fear but accept her messages. The mother of God is mother of us all and would want to come to help us all.

Question: Can you presently recommend the sick in the course of the apparition? Is it possible to ask questions?

Vicka: I do not ask any questions; nevertheless, it is possible to recommend the sick. That is what we do each evening. We intercede on behalf of all the sick and of all those who wander. We present them to Our Lady. We pray in union with her for all the intentions.

Question: During the apparition, does Mary speak to you or rather do you speak to her as well?

Vicka: I say some words from time to time, but not always. She greets first when she arrives. If what she says appears to me obscure, I ask her to explain it to me, and that is what she does. I never ask whatever it may be for myself.

Question: Does she continue to appear to you on a cloud?

Vicka: Yes, exactly as previously.

Question: Have you seen angels since the apparitions?

Vicka: We have seen some sometimes. But only on the Hill of the Apparitions, and on Mt. Krizevac. Never in the church [. . .].

Question: What do the angels resemble?

Vicka: They are all alike to me, some dressed in grey, some in rose; the little angels have wings [. . .].

Question: When will the "Life of the Blessed Virgin" which she has narrated to you be disseminated?

Vicka: As soon as the Gospa asks for it, but she has not yet determined the date [. . .].

Question: Do you have any other special revelations?

Vicka: On the future of the world. But that consists only of two small notebooks [the "Life of the Blessed Virgin" consists of three].

Question: One frequently associates different catastrophes to Medjugorje.

Vicka: The people themselves add much more. Here no one affirms it [. . .]. In our days, people live in anxiety. They create fear for themselves. On their return home, some people who have come here, speak of three days of darkness or of the end of the world, leaving one to understand that it has been said by Mary at Medjugorje. Here, the Queen of Peace has said nothing on this matter. One must live in confidence and not in fear. [. . .]

Question: Our Lady suggests that one offer his life to save the world. In what way do you understand your role with this point of view?

Vicka: The Mother of Jesus has advised this attitude to each one of us under the form of a message. I do not see anything particular in my role [here Vicka's modesty minimizes the total gift which she has made of herself] [. . .].

Question: Have you received messages destined for the group, as in the case for Ivan?

Vicka: No, we perceive the same messages as Ivan; it is his group. Ivan is its leader. Maria and I are frequently on the Hill of the Apparitions when he is there with his group. The Gospa communicates the same messages. But it is Ivan who transmits them because it is he who directs the group [. . .].

Question: Has Mary's face changed in the course of these years? Has she become more aged during these eight years?

Vicka: (laughing)—She is the same. Her face remains the same.

Question: Have you also seen Jesus?

Vicka: We saw Him only once: big, all bruised, with His crown of thorns. It was about four years ago [. . .]. Each Christmas, Mary presents to us the Child Jesus: Baby in her arms.

Question: Do you likewise see the signs: the heart and the cross?

Vicka: When she goes away, we see the cross, the heart, then the sun. At the moment in which she goes away, we see first of all the cross, then the heart and the sun, one after the other. The sun is little: a colored sun [. . .].

Question: Maria reported that Our Lady had once declared to her: "I give you my love so that you can offer it around you." Did she recommend that to all of you?

Vicka: Yes, to each one.

Question: Could you describe for us your relationship with the Queen of Angels? [. . .]

Vicka: I cannot compare that with anyone else, be it my contacts with Mama, Papa, or our conversation with the two of us now. It is unique; it implies love, prayer, dialogue at the same time. I cannot compare it with anything. No!

Question: Have you at times been afraid of the Blessed Virgin?

Vicka: No, never, except the first days, when we were not sure that it was indeed the Gospa.

Question: Each of us sins often. What does that do to you when you meet Our Lady?

Vicka: Yes, we are sinners. But I strive not to sin except in little things. If I would commit a grave sin, I would not advance calmly to the Queen of Peace. I would be ashamed. Nevertheless, I have not yet arrived there.

Question: Is it true that she has frequently recommended: "My children, go to confession now?"

Vicka: Yes [. . .]. If we would understand better, she would not be obliged to remind us; we would know ourselves what we had to do.

Question: According to Ivan, Our Lady insists now on prayer of the heart.

Vicka: Yes, she advises: "Pray with the heart." She adds: "From day to day, open your heart so that prayer may become joy for you, that you pray with love." When we take the Rosary [. . .], she states: "First of all, move aside all thoughts which burden you, then begin to pray!" If you do thusly, [. . .] you will certainly pray with the heart. You will not be looking at your watch to know the time, but you will also pray a long time which your heart will permit you. That is prayer of the heart.

Question: What does the recitation of the Rosary mean for you?

Vicka: It is not a formal obligation. If you perceive it nevertheless in your heart, you will advance so much farther. Then you experience more intensely in your soul. The prayer of the Rosary should transform itself into authentic joy for you. The Gospa affirms that the recitation of the Rosary constitutes the most powerful weapon against Satan. The power of this prayer is so considerable that one can even stop wars, thanks to it.

Question: What would you advise people who have problems with the recitation of the Rosary?

Vicka: These persons should pray slowly, perhaps by limiting themselves first to seven Our Fathers. When you begin to pray with the heart, it will permeate your thought and your soul. We cannot persuade people that they must pray the Rosary. It is necessary for them to really open their hearts and pray with their heart. Thus the Rosary will introduce itself by itself. One does not succeed from the first time.

Question: Does Our Lady recommend to pray for others?

Vicka: Yes, we can pray for others, but always according to the Divine Will, following the desires of the Gospa. She knows what is necessary for us and what others need.

Question: Do you regard Medjugorje as a place from where peace should spread throughout the world?

Vicka: The Gospa specifically states: "I have come as the Queen of Peace and I wish that peace reign on the earth." But we can disseminate harmony abroad. Meanwhile, Our Lady advocates favoring above all, peace in our heart, in our family; then we must pray for harmony in the world. In this way, peace will spread through the intermediary of our prayer [. . .].

Question: You have often said that you would enter the convent when the apparitions would end. Do you discern now that your mission consists in staying in Medjugorje?

Vicka: I must be here. If the Gospa wishes that everything be accomplished to the end, and if she has put me in that place, my mission is to remain there until the complete accomplishment of my task. My duty is to remain here.

Question: How do you find the current development of Medjugorje?

Vicka: Well.

Question: Do you have a plan for the future?

Vicka: Not at this time.

Question: Do these constant visits not cause you any fatigue?

Vicka: No! What could cause me fatigue? There is no problem.

Question: Do you receive enough strength for it?

Vicka: Yes, thanks to God!

Question: How has your family received the flow of pilgrims which have besieged their home for eight years?

Vicka: I am struck with admiration for my family. They have accepted it very well. One of us goes to church every evening. My grandmother is ill [deceased on March 11, 1990], so someone must constantly stay at home. We take turns with my sister and my brother. Each one takes their turn to be at home. And we daily recite the Rosary there.

Question: Doesn't anyone become irritated against the numerous visitors?

Vicka: I am surprised myself at the great patience of my family, because visitors arrive almost every minute. I do not say it only because they are my parents, but they are patient. May God give them the strength!

(*Stella Maris,* October 1989)

N.B.: Another analogous and contemporary interview of Vicka came to us in English. In it, Vicka is asked concerning the end of her trial of health: September 25, 1988 (and not November as was published). In the two interviews, Vicka minimizes her sufferings and does not speak precisely of this state of prostration which her family called her coma. One will find more specific observations in *Eight Years,* pg. 15.

INTERVIEW OF MARIA PAVLOVIC
(August 25, 1989)

Question: Which are the most important messages?

Maria: Those of which the Gospa speaks to us always, that is: prayer, fasting, confession, Holy Mass, and in general, conversion. She asks us to live her messages and to give an example to others in our life. She presents herself to us as the Queen of Peace and asks us to pray for peace so that peace will come into our hearts. And after, the Blessed Virgin told us that if we receive peace into our hearts, we should transmit it to our families surrounding us. And the preferred prayer of the Blessed Virgin is the prayer of the Rosary. If we have peace in our hearts, we will also have it in our families, with our friends, and at that moment we will be able to pray for peace in the whole world, she tells us. Every prayer that is made with the heart pleases God. God should have the first place in our life. She says that it is still necessary to put prayer into our lives.

She asks us to to grow deeper in our prayer from day to day, to increase our prayers from day to day. She also asks us to take special times every day [. . .]. She desires that the 24 hours of our day be prayer because she would like for us to be in contact with God all the time, permanently, even when we work, even when we meet people, to be in contact with God at every moment. It is only thus that we will be able to walk on the path of holiness.

She also tells us that we must fast. Through fasting and prayer we could even stop wars, not only wars which are in the world, but also wars which are in our hearts and in our families. She still says that the best fast is on bread and water. At the beginning, she had asked for a fast only on Friday. Now she had added Wednesday. And if the sick or the old cannot fast on bread and water, the Blessed Virgin asks them to offer their illness. She also asks us to make other sacrifices: that he who smokes, not smoke on that day; he who drinks, not take alcohol on that day. She asks us also to go to confession at least once a month. In this way, we will be able to grow in truth before God and before mankind.

The center of our life must be the Holy Mass [. . .]. We cannot replace Holy Mass with anything. We cannot replace our presence at Holy Mass, for example, by paying for a Mass. She also says: do not look at the people around you at Mass because if you see sinners around you, you are not going to want very much to come to church. Do not look at the priest or at the people around you because it is God directly with Whom you have to deal. The most important thing is our meeting with God and for that the Blessed Virgin also asks us to prepare ourselves for Holy Mass through prayer. In this way, we will be able to make this meeting more profound and stronger with God. That is what the Blessed Virgin speaks to us relentlessly. She wants us to be an example for others by living these messages.

She guides us in a special way through the prayer groups and gives messages for the spiritual growth of these groups.

Those are the most important messages. But you have books where most of this has been written; you will see in them that there are many other messages and we would be able to speak about them for several days. The most important thing for us is to know that it is necessary in this way to walk and grow in the way of faith. (*Oasis,* November 25, 1989)

INTERVIEW OF FR. TOMISLAV VLASIC
(September 1989)

Tomislav was questioned by some twenty young people from the group *Regina Pacis*, from Foggia, at an unspecified date, a little before September 1989.

Question: We are the life and soul of a large prayer group with some hundreds of persons. What do you advise the people who are the life and soul of prayer groups?

Fr. Tomislav: It is difficult to answer. I think that for those who want to guide prayer groups, the essential thing is to find the time for personal and also liturgical prayer. Personal prayer develops the heart. Then, the methods for transferring become simple, because the Gospel is simple and Jesus has shown to us a way of simplicity. The last message of July 25 must be lived by us personally. Only then do we come to be a transparence of God and the Gospa, and it is not very difficult for us to guide the people.

Question: Beyond each one's personal way, can you give some suggestions for prayer groups?

Fr. Tomislav: That depends on the group. It can be some 200 or 20 people [. . .]. Those who wish to advance in spiritual life must learn to maintain silence in order to receive from God, Who manifests Himself particularly in silence. I refer to creative silence in which the individual—joyful, open— prostates himself before God. It is then that God can make miracles. In spiritual life, silence is a condition. If we do not enter into silence, we are always superficial. If we enter it, we become capable of listening to God, understanding God, contemplating God, and then this meeting changes and transforms us [. . .]. Be the group large or small, it must have in it a core of people who go from the beginning, progress, and become the spirit and life, and become a transparence of God. Otherwise, we remain in a closed circle—always many words, many activities, many lessons, and little fruit.

Question: Should this period of silence be only at the personal level or also at the group level?

Fr. Tomislav: Also at the group level. Look, we cannot pray the Rosary without silence. We cannot enter into the mysteries without silence. We cannot listen; we cannot even be a community without silence, because in silence God manifests Himself in a special way in our innermost heart. That means that the community should also find itself there. Not so many words which come from our ego! In groups or in the community, we can call silence "listening": the ability to listen to God but also to our neighbor.

Question: Many observe, nevertheless, that silence in a Eucharistic adoration, for example, is more difficult to live, more weighty than a moment of prayer in an audible voice on the part of him who leads the adoration.

Fr. Tomislav: It is only a sign that we have problems and are afraid to meet with ourselves, because fear which comes to us from silence, is fear of meeting with ourselves and with God. Because of it, silence is a condition, for from within, we can get out our frustrations, our fear, our idols. Without it, with many words, we maintain all our problems, which at times we create, so that our prayers become cries of reaction. A man who speaks from silence and peace is a man of God because he listens always.

Question: In order to be able to meet God in silence, the Gospa invites us to abandon our problems, our concerns. But how does one do it concretely?

Fr. Tomislav: One gets there slowly. That cannot be accomplished in one effort. But it is important to offer, to renounce a negative feeling; for example, to accept a suffering due to being hurt and to forgive. On the moral level, it is a question of offering oneself and of saying: "But, Lord, I accept this situation as it is: I feel myself in a bad situation; I entrust it to You. And I abandon the difficulty and I begin to adore You and to love You!" One of the most tragic things in the spiritual life is that we do not love ourselves when we make a mistake, and do not love others when they make a mistake. Here the tragedy begins. If I do not love myself when I make a mistake, then in the most critical moments of my life, I would not love myself and I would not be able to go on any longer.

Question: When you say "love ourselves," do you mean we should accept ourselves as we are?

Fr. Tomislav: No, to love means actually love ourselves even when we sin, not accepting it but wanting to redeem it. Like a mother when she sees a child fall, runs and embraces him, hugs him, so man should live the love of God in himself and for himself. We have learned to criticize others, to condemn others, and we finish thus by making our own condemnation. Some people, throughout their life, conduct a struggle against themselves and a flight from themselves, and it is a source of tragedy. And our system of preaching is so erroneous that we do not change the situation and the wound remains. For me, the most beautiful pages in the Gospel are those in which Jesus says that there is more rejoicing in Heaven for a sinner who is converted than for 100 just people who do not need conversion. For this, for this situation of sin, when I offer myself to God, I allow the light of the love of God to enter in me. In His Words, we will always find forgiveness, we see how Jesus loves sinners. Then I can meet God in this situation of sin. I begin to adore Him, I leave the problems, and for me it is not more important (to know) if I was, or I am a sinner. What is important is that I live with the love of God and that I meet Him. It is from there that our transformation emanates. (*Eco,* no. 65, p. 5)

The Future

Question: And yet, when we are in sin, sometimes we are discouraged and it is difficult for a positive feeling, like love for ourselves, to come to us after we find ourselves to be miserable sinners.

Fr. Tomislav: That is indeed a problem. Nevertheless, in us there are negative reactions, because we have received the image of a threatening God and it is the aim of Satan to trouble us, to instill fear in us, defiance, incredulity; and then we find ourelves at a standstill. On the contrary, if we Christians were open to meeting with the Resurrected One, we would no longer need psychiatrists.

Question: With respect to Satan, the Gospa says that with the Rosary, the Eucharist, the Gospel, we defeat Satan. And yet, in the life of so many saints, we see that while progressing step by step on the path of holiness, they were threatened, sometimes physically, by the devil. How can those two things be compatible with each other?

Fr. Tomislav: They can be compatible because he who progresses in sanctity always resembles God more, and provokes the wrath of Satan who hates God, and everything that is similar to Him; these people take away many souls from Satan. It is a challenge [. . .] and for that the Gospa, with her children, fight against Satan.

Question: With regard to struggle, do you personally think that we are in the times prophesied by John's Apocalypse?

Fr. Tomislav: Yes, certainly. Of course, because the Word of God speaks with clarity about the revealing signs, and today we have many signs for this present moment of history, many signs not understood, and we should be responsible for them.

Question: Concerning the last times, one has observed that St. Paul was said to already live in the last times. Is this reference prophetic or chronological?

Fr. Tomislav: One can never know what "last times" means. It is a relative term which is found in the Apocalypse, as in the first century of Christianity. But beyond this relative meaning, we must really be aware that we are now in the time of the great events when God wants to work a change for us, and thus the visionaries say that these apparitions are the last for humanity and that with these events the time of Satan is finished. It is true: a new page [has turned], something will come. I ask myself, if Satan will have no more power on earth, what will become of the earth? It can be only love everywhere.

Question: We have read that this power of Satan should be nullified with the accomplishment of the tenth secret: the secret which Mirjana will reveal several days before it occurs.

Then all that is chronologically near, because it will be accomplished in her lifetime. It means the years of the power of Satan are numbered.

Fr. Tomislav: I say no. Before us, there are great events and I would not say before us, but in us. We are already in these events. I spoke a short time ago with a psychiatrist, and I asked him if people were progressing in health, or if illnesses were increasing. He answered me that illnesses were increasing rapidly. The Gospa explained it to us that in moving forward, anxiety in the hearts of men will increase in a continuous manner. This time is a time of anxiety because men have not listened to God, the only One Who can give peace. And with the increase of this anxiety in hearts, we arrive at chaos in us, a universal chaos.

Question: Some among us participate in different ecclesiastic movements and because of the commitment in our prayer group, we encounter some difficulties in these relations. What can we do in order to prove the compatibility between the two commitments?

Fr. Tomislav: It is sufficient to show the fruits. And I think that you are lucky to have people of different movements. God is triune and one. The Trinity is diversity and unity. It has a perfection. Then if you are diverse, and united in love, you are rich and strong because all the movements of the Church are instruments: instruments which must serve one goal of love. And there is someone who can unite these movements, I would say, for a perfect unity—the mother. The mother has no structures; she has love. And you too then, you must be of maternal love for your brothers. Then there will no longer be divisions, but only unity.

Question: In what sense did the Gospa once say: "I have come to purify all movements.?"

Fr. Tomislav: In all movements there is something good and something limited, negative. In my opinion, by "purifying," the Gospa means a relation with God that is more simple, more loving, deeper, and without so many human elements which oppress it. In the face of so many movements, the Madonna presents herself better than anyone with her simple words. In all movements there are theories, methods, structures, leaders. And when all that becomes heavy, then we are in the situation of pharisees who impose burdens on the shoulders of others and people no longer know how to love. I think that in order to arrive at the depth and unity with God, we cannot walk without the Gospa. We believe in the "communion of saints" and we need saints. And the Gospa, beyond the saints, has a role of mother who gives birth to us: for that she has been called "Mother of the Church" and this role is very important. In the Gospa, we do not find either theories or structures, but always the mother who gives birth and prepares for the gifts of the Holy Spirit. Despite the fears that the Madonna can be an obstacle on the way of ecumenical dialogue, we have discovered the contrary: the Gospa is unique; she unites because she does not need these theories, but loves each one like a mother. At the same time, she represents the love of God and then through her, we can touch God, experience God. (*Eco,* no. 65, p. 5-6)

Consecration

Question: In order to be united to this unique mother, one often speaks of consecration. Could you explain to us how we must understand this term?

Fr. Tomislav: There are several steps in consecration: consecration in the broad sense (to which the Gospa calls) and the consecration of life according to the practice of the Church, as when a person consecrates themself completely as a religious, a nun or layman, in a consecrated community. First, it is through consecration that we try to be the most similar to the Blessed Virgin, to her Immaculate Heart, to develop in us her very virtues. The second point is that by consecrating ourselves, we offer our freedom to the Blessed Virgin and then she has the responsibility of protecting us against Satan.

One more point: consecration has been announced in a particular way for these times. The triumph of the Immaculate Heart means that these times belong to the Gospa and as she said to us, in certain messages: "The time will come when, without my protection, you will not be able to go forward." During these times, when we await the triumph of the Immaculate Heart, God has given a special role to the Gospa. On offering ourselves to her, we live this reality in preparation for the triumph of her Immaculate Heart, which will also be the triumph of our hearts.

Then there is the meaning of consecration within a community. It is another step. When people totally offer themselves to God through the Immaculate Heart, in order to live only for God twenty-four hours a day, it is a call to give everything to the Gospa in order to increase this triumph. One offers oneself as an instrument for this triumph.

Question: Sometimes you have spoken of "volunteer victim" [the community of Tomislav was oriented to this sacrifice]. What does that mean exactly?

Fr. Tomislav: The "volunteer victim" is the last step in the program of the Gospa because one reaches the highest grade in the love for God and for one's neighbor—to give everything for God and to give everything for one's brother, while preparing oneself to suffer, to take upon himself the consequences of the sins of his brothers, to save the world. And yet, in order to understand it, it is necessary to see what precedes. First of all, a purification is necessary, an increase of love in the persons who really become in love with God: like a mother is ready to watch all night in order to hold the child. The mother does not suffer in her heart when she helps the little one, even if she must stand watch all night. Inwardly she is happy when she sees the child happy with her. And indeed, in these souls which offer themselves, there is this love. The Gospa wants to develop this love so that the difficulties and the sufferings are no longer sufferings. And it is always a way to the resurrection, to the extent that we are ready to take upon us these sufferings of Christ and our brothers. In this way the sins of our brothers are burned in us. The Gospa wants for people in these communities to live this love above everything among themselves, and for the salvation of the world.

Question: What does the Gospa mean in the message where she says: "Have an active conscience?"

Fr. Tomislav: The active conscience is nothing else than a continuous attention so that God, Who receives us at Mass and in His Word, may be kept, protected, be the object to our cares. And thus the joy which we receive is protected.

Active conscience is not understood then in the sense of "activism"; it would be contrary to the attitude of the Gospa, because it is God Who is active in us.

INTERVIEW OF IVAN DRAGICEVIC
(October, 1989)

Question: How did you live interiorly the day which followed the first apparition?

Ivan: The first day for me was the twenty-fifth [on the twenty-fourth he hardly saw, from a distance, and ran off]. It was something very difficult to experience, for it was a terrible shock and we asked ourselves what was happening to us, if we were on earth, in Heaven, if we were alive, and we did not know any longer anything of where we were. This shock lasted for all the visionaries at least 6 months, and we were afraid of what was happening to us. And the Blessed Virgin got us used to her presence little by little, and we developed a personal relationship with her in great depth. This makes it easier for me now to speak to the Blessed Virgin than to speak to you.

Question: What important things does one stress in the last message [that of July 25, two months before]?

Ivan: The Gospa asks us to pray as families. She says that the family should be the place where holiness is born. Holiness is not only for the monks! It is for everybody, for the young and the families.

Since the last apparition on the hill last Monday, she asked us to live her messages, to put them into practice in our lives. She added: "If you do not live the messages which I have given, I cannot give you any new messages." We are very desirous of receiving new messages. Undoubtedly you too, like everybody, but the Blessed Virgin tells us that we cannot receive other messages if we do not live those which we have already received. That is what she said the last time that she appeared to me on the hill.

People do not understand what it means to receive a message. That means to live it. If you do not live it, well then, it does not make any sense [. . .]. First of all, it is necessary to know how to live the present message and not be greedy to always receive new messages. It is very important [. . .].

Question: It seems that the Blessed Virgin does not give a very positive picture of television.

Ivan: The Gospa asks us to curb our freedoms, for television in particular. It does not mean that it is necessary to leave out television completely. But it is up to parents to discern which programs there are which their children can watch and which there are which they cannot watch.
(*Oasis*, October 1989)

INTERVIEW OF IVAN DRAGICEVIC
(October 30, 1989)

Before they asked questions, Ivan spoke to the pilgrims these words:

Ivan: The most important thing is to know what the Blessed Virgin asks of us; it is to follow the messages which she gives us, that is to say, peace, prayer, conversion, penance. It is necessary to live all that the Blessed Virgin tells us in these messages. Follow it with the heart, and the message dearest to the Blessed Virgin is prayer of the heart. That is the most important message!

Question: What does it mean to pray with the heart?

Ivan: To pray with the heart means to pray and to know what one is praying, that is, everything that one is saying, to think about it without thinking of anything else. To pray with the heart means to think about what one is saying inwardly. It is true that to start is always difficult, it is hard. Today everybody has difficulties and that can make us deviate. No one is perfect. To pray with the heart is life. With prayer one succeeds in forgetting his problems. It is the only thing that will help you to solve them.

The most important thing is for man to decide to pray. Let him make the great decision to pray. It is necessary to decide this act, to want it.

Afterwards it is peace. It is important for everyone. It is

necessary to have peace everywhere in the world. It is necessary to have peace with oneself, peace in the Church. That is important because it is we who make the Church [. . .].

The Blessed Virgin calls for the reconversion of everything evil in our lives, of all negative things. It is necessary to eliminate them. It is necessary that we live a better way in our lives, and on this way we will find God; His presence is very near to us.

Question: Is it better to read the Word, that is, the Gospel, or to become oriented more toward prayer?

Ivan: For prayer groups everything is necessary: the Gospel, meditation, discussion among the people, even a walk, so that it may not be monotonous.

Question: Does the Blessed Virgin really ask of us lay people that we are to say a full Rosary a day or pray three hours a day?

Ivan: We have the time. However, it is the quality which counts, and not the quantity.

INTERVIEW OF JELENA VASILJ
(End of 1989)

Question: What is your daily life like?

Jelena: The greatest part of my time presently is taken by nursing school in Mostar. I begin the day with prayer as a family, and I attend Mass almost every evening. Three times a week, our prayer group meets after Mass. Each day I also have my personal prayer. I have no set time for that, but I pray spontaneously when I have the time to speak to God.

Question: How has Our Lady helped your life of faith?

Jelena: Everything began on December 29, 1982, when I was only 10 years old. During a biology class in school, for the first time, I heard the voice of an angel. And it returned for several days. Very soon he told me that I would hear Our Lady. I heard her voice and I see her interiorly. That was the beginning of my spiritual growth, my whole life changed [. . .].

Question: Was it Our Lady who asked you to form a prayer group?

Jelena: Yes, it was in 1983. Fr. Vlasic became our director. Later, a small group was formed from the large group. Our Lady asked us to devote three hours a day to prayer and to fast twice a week. She wanted each of us to do so. We pray in different ways in our meetings. Often we read Holy Scripture, especially the Gospels. We meditate on the messages which Our Lady gives us; we often say the Rosary together. We pray spontaneously or we meditate [. . .].

Question: Can you tell us your personal experience of Our Lady?

Jelena: I have the apparitions almost every day. I see her in an interior way, through the heart. And I can hear what she tells me. It never happens outside of prayer, deep prayer. She has never given me messages for myself personally. She told me that her messages were for everyone. I have a very strong experience of her direction even when she gives me a warning. She is like a very tender mother. (*Medjugorje messenger). Jelena will be 19 years old on May 14, 1991.*

INTERVIEW OF JELENA VASILJ BY GIUSEPPE MINTO
(End of 1989)

G. Minto: Jelena, when did you begin to see the Gospa?

Jelena: When I was in school, I heard a voice which told me to pray. When my friends and I began to form a prayer group, at the end of a few days, I began to see the Gospa. I believed immediately. But even now it is difficult for me to think that the Gospa comes to me; it is an impossible thing to explain.

G. Minto: Do you still see her?

Jelena: Yes, every day.

G. Minto: How do you see her?

Jelena: Not physically but interiorly (with the heart).

G. Minto: When do you ordinarily see her?

Jelena: In prayer.

G. Minto: And what do you experience?

Jelena: A great peace, a great joy.

G. Minto: You have also seen Jesus.

Jelena: Yes, at Christmas, twice.

G. Minto: We know that you lead a prayer group.

Jelena: No, it is the Gospa who leads it!

G. Minto: How did you begin?

Jelena: The Gospa asked us: Do you want to form a prayer group? And we said yes.

G. Minto: How does your prayer group function?

Jelena: The Gospa and Jesus are like teachers. They give messages, and if we do not understand, they will explain them. In the group there are spontaneous prayers and meditations, and we speak about God because the world and our parish need to hear about God. Jesus gives us messages, then explains. We also pray the Rosary.

G. Minto: How long do the meetings of your group last?

Jelena: Sometimes an hour, sometimes two, and when we have the time, up to four hours [. . .].

G. Minto: What does the Gospa say?

Jelena: She always says to pray, that prayer will bring us peace and the certainty of God. When we pray, it is peaceful.

G. Minto: Jelena, is faith a gift?

Jelena: Yes, but it is necessary to receive it in prayer. When we pray, to believe is not so difficult, but when one does not pray, we easily get lost in this world. It is necessary to understand that the devil wants to detach us from God. It is necessary to believe and also to put into practice our faith. It is necessary to believe with all our heart.

G. Minto: Do you fast?

Jelena: Twice and at times three times a week, on bread and water.

G. Minto: Do you have a plan for your life?

Jelena: No, I do not think about tomorrow.

G. Minto: What must one do in order to know the will of God for us?

Jelena: For that it is necessary to pray. If we worry too much, it is a mistake. The Lord does everything through us. Also we must only pray and entrust ourselves into His hands. You understand in prayer what the Lord wants from you [. . .].

G. Minto: What should we tell the sick?

Jelena: To see Jesus in their cross and in this way to recognize Him, because the Gospa says that the Cross helps us to come closer to Him.

G. Minto: And what does the Gospa say of this world?

Jelena: The Gospa does not say anything specific, but she knows everything. (Interview published in *Medjugorje Torino*, January-February, 1990)

INTERVIEW OF MARINKO
Protector of the Visionaries During the First Months
(End of 1989)

I have often questioned Marinko, first-class witness, born in 1943, an auto mechanic who changed his profession to receiving pilgrims. For this, he built a large boarding house. We extract this account from the interview published by *Medjugorje Torino* (No. 30). These are some less known and more significant characteristics.

Marinko: Maria Pavlovic was the first to speak to me of the apparitions of the Blessed Virgin on the morning of June 25, 1981, while I drove her, with Vicka Ivankovic, to Citluk for their summer classes. In the afternoon of the same day, I went to look for Ivan Dragicevic. Later, I went to the place of the apparitions, but arrived too late, for I thought that it was 7:15 in the evening and it was 6:15. That was June 26. I accompanied and helped the visionaries for the first time on the Hill of the Apparitions. I continued in the best as well as the worst times.

Krazevic: Marinko, how did you come into contact with the group of visionaries?

Marinko: I used to attend the weekly retreats of reflection on marriage. I am a practicing Catholic. I was sensitive to the situation of the visionaries. Ivanka's mother had died and her father was in Germany. Jakov's father lived in Bosnia and rarely came. Mirjana's family lived in Sarajevo. These young people did not sufficiently have the protection of their parents. I had to help them [. . .]. They had more faith in me than in any other person.

Krazevic: More than in the Franciscan fathers?

Marinko: Of course, because they did not go to the apparitions and did not allow themselves to be seen.

Krazevic: Were you the first to report it to the priests in the parish?

Marinko: Yes, the second day; I was even late. When I arrived on the hill of Podbrdo, I saw that the young people were coming down from the hill. They already had the apparition. Ivanka was accompanied by her grandmother; Ivanka was troubled and crying. Then she embraced her grandmother and said while sobbing: "Grandmother, I asked the Gospa for news of my mother and she told me that she was all right, she was in paradise." I tried to calm her down but I was not successful. She continued to cry. Then I decided to go to the priests and tell them what had taken place [. . .]. I went to the presbytery. Two sisters were on the stairs. I asked them if there was a priest in the house: "Yes, Father Zrinko," said one of them. I would have preferred Father Jozo, but I reported the events to Zrinko. He told me: "Marinko, those who say they see, they see; and those who do not see, they do not see." I returned home.

Krazevic: What did you think of these remarks of Father Zrinko?

Marinko: I did not think he was right, but who could discuss it with him? I would have wanted for him to come with me to see the young people, to speak with them [. . .]. I did not succeed in understanding why he had not wanted to come with me. It was as though it did not matter anything to him that the Madonna appeared. I could not understand his indifference. That seemed to me inconceivable [. . .].

The continuation of the interview narrates the first contacts (very well known) of Dragika, Marinko's wife, with Fr. Jozo Zovko. They were thus the first to inform the clergy. Zrinko narrates then the luminous sign which he perceived on the hill 20 days after the first apparition. That would have been July 10, toward 11 p.m. This is another fact already known.

Krazevic: Do you remember other events?

Marinko: Once I was called by Jakov and Vicka. They were going to have an apparition in Vicka's home, in her room. Some children were there with me singing religious hymns. Jakov said: "Marinko, come with us." I went with my son Dabor and another child, Matan Sego. On climbing the stairs to Vicka's home, we slowed down and entered the house after the two visionaries. All of a sudden, Jakov called: "Marinko, the Gospa is there!"

That happened two days before the trial of Fr. Jozo [autumn, 1981]. I climbed the last two steps of the staircase of the court-yard and I fell on my knees at the door without daring to advance any further. Behind me, my son and Matan fell on their knees. I stretched out my hand and said this prayer: "Dear Gospa, prove now or never to those who do not believe that our Jozo is innocent." I did not pay any attention to the colloquy of Jakov and Vicka with the Gospa. I simply said this sentence. Now, the visionaries spoke to me: "The Gospa is smiling at you; she is coming toward you; she is there. She is embracing you; she is enveloping you in her arms. She is blessing you." I experienced a very strong, unexplainable feeling. The visionaries continued: "The Madonna is saying to you: 'Marinko, do not lose your faith, persevere in your faith.'" Then I said: "I am not afraid to give my life for Jesus but show me the way to follow." This was the first response which came to me from the spirit. Then the visionaries turned toward the place where the Gospa was; Jakov and Vicka repeated to me the words of the Gospa: "Watch these children who glorify me." I thought she was referring to the children who were with me at first in my house, and who were singing religious hymns. Jakov and Vicka continued: "The Madonna asks you to lead here *all* the children." The children [. . .] arrived, also my sister-in-law. They advanced as far as the door. Jakov and Vicka turned again and said: "The Madonna is over you and blesses all of you." Thus the evening ended.

(Marinko then narrates the best known episode of the apparition in the field of Gumno, August 2, 1981).

Some people touched the Blessed Virgin, but her robe became stained where some had touched it. Maria told me: "Oh, Marinko, when the Gospa left us, her robe was all stained and black!" I asked her: "Why was it stained black?" Maria answered that there were some people, some sinners, and when they touched her, her robe became black and dirty. Then she asked all those who were present to go to confession as soon as possible.

I stayed a little bit longer to speak with Maria. Thus I learned that, that evening, on returning from the church, she had gone to her house to change before going to the fields and alone had an apparition from the Gospa in her room. From this apparition, she told me: "This evening, the Gospa explained to me: It is even here that the devil tries to infiltrate. He tries at all cost to attain his glory. But My Son wants to attract all souls to Him. The devil tries to prevent Him; he struggles to infiltrate at all cost in your midst." (*Medjugorje Torino*).

INTERVIEW OF MIRJANA DRAGICEVIC SOLDO
by Jan Connell, Portland, Oregon
(February 2, 1990)

Question: Mirjana, what did you feel when the Blessed Virgin told you she would no longer appear to you each day?

Mirjana: I was so depressed that I did not want to believe it. I felt so separated from Our Lady that I felt my heart was breaking. I knelt down and began to pray and to pray, but she did not appear and I prayed more. I wished only to die, to look for Heaven rather than this life without the presence of Our Lady. At the end of six days, Our Lady appeared and explained to me that she would no longer come regularly. She promised to appear to me every year for my birthday on March 18, and at certain times in my life when I would go through serious difficulties with respect to the secrets which had been given to me. She prepared me to live in the world like everyone.

Question: Do you continue to hear the voice of Our Lady?

Mirjana: When I pray, I experience her very near.

Question: Why do you hear her the second day of each month now?

Mirjana: Our Lady promised me that she would appear to me at a time when I would need her in a special way. She told me that she wants to appear to me for the revelation of the secrets, which she has entrusted to me. Sometimes, I maintain the weight of the secrets with difficulty. Then the Blessed Virgin comes to me, encourages me and she strengthens me on the matter of these secrets which she has revealed to me.

Question: Are these secrets so terrible that Our Lady must strengthen you and help you?

Mirjana: If Our Lady did not help me, I would not be able to bear them; it is so hard for me! At the same time, she has told me that I must not, that we should not be frightened. We must accept God as our Father and Mary as our Mother. We must only concentrate ourselves on the unfathomable love of God for us. He desires above all to save His poor sinning children.

Question: What do we have to do?
Mirjana: To follow Jesus, to walk on earth to the extended arms of Our Father.
Question: Why is Our Lady so sad these days?
Mirjana: Because many do not listen to her messages. Many continue to waste their precious time on earth by living only for the things which pass. Many waste their time looking on that which does not have eternal value.

INTERVIEW OF VICKA IVANKOVIC
by Jan Connell
(March 7, 1990)

Question: Vicka, do you think that the apparitions are going to stop very soon?
Vicka: I do not know.
Question: Do you know why she appears here?
Vicka: Yes, I know why. She would like to lead all of us to Heaven. We do not understand how much the Virgin Mary loves each of us and how much she desires for each of us to know her as a mother. She asks us to pray for one another with her; she always intercedes for each of us. We have to pray for one another like children. Prayer groups have great effectiveness. If only we would know how much it pleases God to see all His children on their knees before Him, with the Mother of Heaven who has given us her Son Jesus! If only we would understand the power of intercession which is the prayer the Virgin Mary has, we would be very happy! There would be no more wars if all entrusted their problems to God. Families would live in great peace, in great harmony if they prayed and fasted and submitted all their problems to God through the Blessed Virgin Mary. Mary is our mother of Heaven.
Question: Vicka, what do you recommend?
Vicka: There is a parable which says: Bloom where you are planted. If everyone blossoms where God plants him, the world would be beautiful and holy. But each one does not

do so; many cease to bloom. There are so many there who do not want to blossom where they have been planted. They reject God's plan over them.

Question: Do you have anything else to share with us?

Vicka: Yes, what the Blessed Virgin wishes: pray for the young people because they are really in a very, very difficult situation. The only way to help them is with your prayers from your hearts. What the world offers young people today will pass quickly. Through what the world offers them, we can see that Satan utilizes every moment, every opportunity to destroy. The best way for Satan to be effective is to exercise an influence over the young people, to infiltrate the families that the young who marry will form.

Question: Why?

Vicka: He does not want for anyone to have the experience of love.

Question: What is the best way to fight against Satan's plan? What has the Blessed Virgin said?

Vicka: The best armor against Satan is prayer and fasting.

INTERVIEW OF JAKOV COLO
by Jan Connell
(March 7, 1990)

Question: Jakov, can you describe your apparition of each day?

Jakov: Yes, the coming of the Gospa is preceded by a brilliant light which comes three times. Then the Gospa appears and she always says: "Praised be Jesus." Afterwards, I greet her. I recommend the sick who come here. Then she and I pray together.

Question: What prayers do you say together?

Jakov: The "Our Father," the "Glory Be," and other prayers of our heart to God.

Question: What does our good Mother resemble? Is there a word that comes to you from the spirit?

Jakov: The Mother of Jesus is pure love. The love which

she has is not only for me but for each one in the whole world.

Question: How do you know?

Jakov: During these years with the Gospa, I have experienced it.

Question: Do you know your future?

Jakov: The Gospa has taught me very much about it.

Question: What is your relationship to her? A mother, a friend, a confidant?

Jakov: It is very difficult to find words to describe this relationship. I am her child; I am a messenger in God's plan.

Question: Can you say some things about your daily apparitions?

Jakov: Yes, I have a special place in my house where I pray, at a place where the Gospa appears to me. Every day I begin the Rosary at 6 in the evening; at 6:40 the Gospa arrives.

Question: Do you always begin the Rosary at home at this place?

Jakov: Yes, most evenings. But sometimes I go to church. Then the Gospa appears to me in church.

Question: Do you know whether you will go to Heaven when you die?

Jakov: I have already been to Heaven. [The visit which Our Lady had him make on November 12, 1981.]

Question: Is it difficult to live on earth after having been to Heaven?

Jakov: I would not like to speak about my sufferings.

INTERVIEW OF FR. JOZO ZOVKO
by the *National Catholic Register*
(March 26, 1990)

Jozo Zovko, 49 years of age in 1990, was the pastor in Medjugorje at the time of the first apparitions until his imprisonment in August 1981. Gifted with great spiritual charisms (catechesis, prophecy, conversions, cures), he receives many pilgrims to his parish of Tihaljina (approximately 40 kilometers from Medjugorje) and comes twice a week to Medjugorje to give two hours of information to pilgrims in Italian, English, and German.

Question: What do you think of the run-away commercialization of Medjugorje?

Fr. Zovko: It is not only the problem of tourist agencies. Believe it or not, it is better now than before. You cannot imagine all that we had to confront in this area.

Recently a lot of squatter's shops had to be removed from the road which leads to the church. These merchants came from everywhere. Some were Muslims, some unbelievers, etc. Whether they sold rosaries or Bibles, they did not feel the least responsibility toward the people; as far as they were concerned, it was only business.

But the Church is not a police; we cannot drive away those people. The Church does not have the means to protect itself from developments such as these. I know pilgrims want to take back some souvenirs from Medjugorje with them, that is understandable, but I feel more in agreement with the people who want to take back with them simple things like a rock or some thyme gathered on the Hill of the Apparitions, something free.

Question: Government officials say that they are going to limit future developments of business, that an official overall plan for Medjugorje will be quickly applied. Will that help?

Fr. Zovko: The village is already disfigured and who is now going to destroy all these permanent shops built very close to the parish church? From the beginning, we Franciscans had suggested plans to set up shops in a special zone, but the government continued to give new permits to construct shops near key sites. At the beginning, it was easier for the people of the village to recognize the authorities as the enemy. Now the people are not so sure. And we must understand that all of this commercialism is against Medjugorje, against the messages and against what Medjugorje should be. I am truly angry about it. One day I took along a group of priests to the Hill of the Apparitions to pray; at the top I was able to hear the noise of hammers and construction engines. For me it was like Calvary; I thought I was hearing the noise of the nails being forced into the hands of Christ.

Question: Many participants of charismatic renewal are supporters of Medjugorje. Do you see a connection between Medjugorje and charismatic renewal?

Fr. Zovko: No direct connection. All those who are open can receive grace and a renewal of faith which flow from Medjugorje. For more than eight years Our Lady has succeeded in her call to prayer. The movements of renewal are principally movements of prayer. That is why these other movements recognize a harmony with Medjugorje, a convergence of goals. Medjugorje is not only a purely human movement, for it deals with the presence of God, truth and grace, for all those who look toward Him.

Question: But Medjugorje is often described by its friends and enemies as a phenomenon of charismatic renewal.

Fr. Zovko: I do not know how many people in the village know charismatic renewal even today. Not at all in 1981. At that time, none of the visionaries knew how to pray the Rosary. No charismatic renewal was present at that time. And for that matter now. The visionaries did not have any personal connections among themselves.

When people began to look for ways to destroy Medjugorje, they came upon the idea that the visionaries stemmed from charismatic prayer groups and that the apparitions were a product of them. When they advanced that, it was as if one considered our people as spiritual orphans who had to produce their certificate of spiritual origin. In Medjugorje, we have today a devotion which has always been among us: Our Lady.

Our goal is not to form prayer groups abroad but to develop prayer in the family. Whoever thinks that there is a direct link between Medjugorje and the charismatics does not know our history and our local mentality.

Question: From the historical point of view, do you see any connection between the past events in Croatia and the apparitions?

Fr. Zovko: Yes, but not in the manner in which one would think. Medjugorje was not born because of our history or because of the charismatic movement (which was born from a certain death in the Church and from the spiritual emptiness in the West). Medjugorje comes from Heaven. It is a pure gift from God. That is why it was difficult for me to accept it at the beginning. That is why it is hard for our bishop, Monsignor Zanic, to accept it, because it calls for change.

Unless a person accepts change, the message of Medjugorje appeals to your soul like a beggar. Medjugorje calls you to relieve you of all your presuppositions and to begin a new approach to things, a radically new way. Medjugorje does not produce pharisees.

Question: Pharisees?

Fr. Zovko: He who says: I listen but I will not act. If I say, "I love Our Lady, but I do not pray the Rosary as she has asked," well then, there is the challenge of Medjugorje! It is not what you think about the apparitions that is important, but what you are going to do personally, in life. Our Lady asks you to take her in your hands. That is why many people miss experiencing this on their pilgrimage to Medjugorje. They want to examine things in a physical, intellectual manner, even though Medjugorje is a confrontation of the soul with God.

Question: But do you see any connection between Yugoslav history and the apparitions?

Fr. Zovko: Of course. Religion is the frontier between East and West. Christians here have always been persecuted in two directions. First of all, each enemy of the Cross established itself on the land. Our land was sprinkled with the blood of many martyrs. That is perhaps why the miracle which we call Medjugorje came here. Perhaps Our Lady decided now to honor this history in a special way.

The gift which is Medjugorje should go elsewhere. We are happy and grateful that she has chosen us to call the Church of our generation to a renewal through this miracle. It is not strange that this should be the way. After all, Jesus formulated for the whole world, on a small hill in Galilee, the Sermon of the Mount.

Question: Do you think that there is a connection between the message of peace given by Mary in Medjugorje and the spirit of the movements of reform in eastern Europe?

Fr. Zovko: Yes, I think that in history this is the time of Our Lady. The last years of our century belong to her in a very special way. And who do we see today in eastern Europe? The persons who imprisoned people yesterday, preach freedom today. He who destoyed life works today to build it. It is not only the fact of the insufficiency of the Communist system; it is the grace which works in history. The West should not think of these movements as a profit and loss situation. It is a mistake to think in this manner. You see, we think that Gorbachev is a great man. We are deeply grateful to him. We know that his mother is an Orthodox Christian. And she prays for him every day. What is happening today in eastern Europe is not a defeat for a few; it is a victory for grace.

INTERVIEW OF IVAN JURICI
Secretary of the Government for Tourism
in the Region of Citluk-Medjugorje
(March 1990)

This interview was obtained by the journalist Gabriel Meyer, of the *National Catholic Register* (March 25, 1990). The Secretary of the Communist Party of Citluk (county seat on which Medjugorje depends), put in charge by the Communist government of the problems of urbanization and tourism of Medjugorje, gives these numbers: Medjugorje totals nearly a quarter of all the Yugoslav tourism ($400 million of $2 billion).

Question: What is the official attitude of the Communist Party concerning the events in Medjugorje?

Jurici: It is simple; the Church is responsible for the pilgrims and has the freedom to concern itself with the religious dimension.

Question: But that has not always been the case.

Jurici: It is true. At first we doubted that the Church could cultivate the phenomenon in order to develop a political sentiment. You must understand it; all that was a surprise and shock. Almost no one knew what to do.

Question: When did you hear about Medjugorje for the first time?

Jurici: I heard about it the fifth day [of the apparitions]. The government, like myself, was confronted with many questions. For example, at the beginning, at least 5,000 persons from outside of Medjugorje came to the hill each day. How did such a crowd come so quickly? All questions of law and order were asked. It was normal for the authorities to be concerned about it. The matter was all the more sensitive for it implied matters in dispute between Church and State.

We saw there was a real problem, and we tried an approach of good sense in order to avoid a serious rupture in the relations with the Church. The relations were very strained at that time. There was a great distrust. The authorities were tempted to treat the problem of Medjugorje radically, to suppress it, and to do everything necessary to stop it.

The continuation of the events went very quickly. Suddenly, we had a world center of pilgrimage on our hands. First of all, the Italians came, followed by the Austrians. Since the beginning, this whole matter seemed out of control.

Question: The key was to find a common approach between the government and the Church, was it not?

Jurici: Yes.

Question: The common approach was economic, was it not?

Jurici: Actually [. . .], the government could have avoided a lot of problems for itself if it had understood that you cannot control things such as that, if it had accepted it, if it had assumed its proper role in the situation.

Question: And that role is?

Jurici: Treat the pilgrims properly, maintain good streets, establish telephone lines and other similar things.

Question: The old Minister of Religious Affairs, Filip Simic, would have said, one is sure, that there were nationalistic Croatian provocations on the mountain of Krizevac during the first days of the apparition, and that the authorities were scared of them. Is it true?

Jurici: There were no incidents of this kind at Medjugorje, but you must understand how sensitive things were. When the Croatians began a nationalistic activism, the government was subjected to an escalation of problems with the other nationalities. Such tensions are a serious concern for the Yugoslav state. It is the responsibility of the government to try to de-escalate nationalistic sentiments, and to avoid giving the impression that the government favors them.

Question: How would you describe the situation here today?

Jurici: The Church carries on its own business without interference, and the political community considers, as its responsibility, to create a normal tourist situation with the normal services for the comfort of visitors.

Question: How has Medjugorje changed?

Jurici: In 1981, in the whole region of Medjugorje, there were a total of only 18 bathrooms in all the homes. Today there are more than 4,000. There is a higher standard of living.

Question: What about construction?

Jurici: Between 1981 and 1985, there was tension between the government and the Church concerning Medjugorje. During this period, there was no control over construction. Private owners built what they wanted without qualification.

In my opinion, if there had been a plan, the area around the parish church would have been protected. The merchants want to take advantage of the pilgrims. During the first years, none of the shops were authorized. Now we have begun to deal in a more constructive manner with the situation. The current task is to bring enough water and electricity to Medjugorje. And we want to see the local population and the authorities work together in order to find solutions to these problems.

The investments must be at the same time both private and public. My greatest concern is to plan the drainage system. If there is no adequate drainage with all these pilgrims, a potential epidemic would be there. In any case, we try to channel the property taxes in Medjugorje. For example, the organization of streets which you see around the church come from taxes on property.

Question: Where do the merchants come from?

Jurici: The merchants come from the village and from the outside. Many merchants who have come from the outside stay among the people in the village. Last year, the majority of the merchants were gypsies; there was no license; it was an unpleasant spectacle. Fortunately, we have been able to get rid of all of these.

Our idea for the future is to build a market outside of the center of Medjugorje. We are drawing a comprehensive plan for Medjugorje in which each item will be arranged. The plan should be made public in March [1990].

Question: What about agriculture in Medjugorje?

Jurici: We feel the need to preserve the fundamental character of Medjugorje as an agricultural area. We realize that many things have been done which cannot be undone. But we will try to put in order everything that has been done, especially to preserve the oldest historical houses. As officials of the local government, we are definitely against over-construction in Medjugorje and against large five-story-type structures that would ruin the environment.

And we have learned something in the course of the years. The pilgrims want close contact with the people of the village; the commercial element hinders it.

Question: But some of the problems which you mention would seem to call for immediate attention.

Jurici: The authorities do not have enough money for quick solutions. There is the problem. Drainage is an example. If there were any epidemic here, everyone would blame the government. But I tell my colleagues in the government: why do we not invest more in Medjugorje? Now, because of the growth of tourism, I reasonably trust that we will obtain more funds from the regional and federal government than before. You must understand it: religious tourism is something new here. It is well understood in places like the Holy Land, but it is something new for us.

The parish has understood that and it has given important help to the government in order to construct the bridge and a larger access route to Medjugorje.

Question: With respect to religious tourism, what is the importance of the pilgrimage of Medjugorje in the Yugoslav annual economy?

Jurici: The figures of the Official Yugoslav Tourism show that the pilgrims to Medjugorje alone produced approximately $400 million a year for the Yugoslav economy.

Last year the total tourist income in Yugoslavia was $2 billion. That means that Medjugorje constitutes approximately one fifth of the total tourist revenue of the country. And you will be impressed that all that takes place in a socialist country.

INTERVIEW OF JAKOV
by Dom Pietro Zorza, recorded by A. M. Soro,
transcribed by A. Bonifacio (excerpt)
(April 13, 1990)

Zorza: What do you remember of the first day—June 25, 1981? [. . .]

Jakov: I have never thought that anything of this nature would take place. At that moment I had at the same time both fear and great joy. On the first day we prayed with the Gospa. Ivanka requested to know where her mother was. We did not request anything. We had a great joy and we were crying [from emotion] during this apparition.

Zorza: During this daily meeting, how do you experience the Gospa?

Jakov: We experience her as a mother and each day we have greater joy to see her. We can speak with the Gospa about everything. She is better than our mother. We can say everything and she always helps.

Zorza: Vicka said that you began to cry when the Gospa suggested to you that she would take you to see Paradise, Purgatory, and Hell.

Jakov: I never speak of that. I was afraid because it was a strange thing for me and I was so young. How old was I—12 or 13? [It was on November 12, 1981; he was then 10 or 11 years.] I said to the Gospa, "Gospa, take Vicka for she still has seven brothers and sisters, but I am an only son." But the Gospa said that we should not be afraid because she was with us. And after that we went there.

Zorza: But why did the Gospa make you see that? [. . .]

Jakov: We saw Paradise, Purgatory, and Hell. The Gospa wanted us to see that it exists also. In Paradise we saw many people who were praying, who were speaking together; later, in Purgatory, we saw only like a cloud and inwardly something was moving. I do not want to speak about Hell [. . .]. Hell exists; I have seen it. Perhaps before, I had some doubts about those things. But now, I know that they really exist. [. . .]

Zorza: You have said that those who were in Paradise were praying and speaking. [...]

Jakov: I did not hear, I only saw that the people were praying. I did not hear what they prayed or what they said.

Zorza: Why fasting? [...]

Jakov: The Gospa recommends fasting two days each week: Wednesday and Friday. Once she said that with prayer and fasting one can do everything, even stop wars. [...]

Zorza: When you speak with her, does she answer you, help you, or rather make you hear the answer through the heart?

Jakov: The Gospa answers me and helps me. [...] Sometimes, when I do not ask for anything and also when I make a mistake, she tells me or helps me to understand that such a thing is not good. [...]

Zorza: What has she asked of you these later times?

Jakov: The Gospa told me (I do not remember when) that we must pray very much for sinners, who are still very numerous. And on March 20, when she told me that I would not have any apparitions for ten days, she also told me that during this time, I should pray very much for her intentions. I think then that we must pray very much at this time for the Gospa's intentions.

Zorza: Are you afraid that it will end?

Jakov: Yes, indeed! Because we have been with the Gospa for such a long time, and we have gotten used to it. I would like for it to last always.

Zorza: And the future of the world?

Jakov: Yes, the Gospa told me about the future of the world, but for the time being, I am not able to say anything about it.

Zorza: And fasting?

Jakov: The Gospa tells us that we must fast on bread and water. But there are many sick; the Gospa tells them that on that day they should pray. And then, there are indeed other ways to fast: for example, not to smoke, not to watch television...give up something which we use every day.

Zorza: The Gospa always says to pray. But does she not also say to act?

Jakov: Yes. She also says to do good.

Zorza: She wants this year, for the family, to be the center of our concerns [. . .].

Jakov: [. . .] We prayed together as a family, but later, when the Gospa said that we should pray, it is the evening that we pray as a family. Now, for example, and during Lent, we have prayed each evening three Jesus Rosaries. And after Lent, we always pray the Rosary, the seven "Our Fathers," "Hail Marys," and "Glory Be."

Zorza: Many Italians have lost the habit of going to Mass. What is the value of the Mass?

Jakov: I have understood that the Mass must be the center of our lives.

Zorza: You are privileged by the Madonna, and yet you are deprived of your parents. [. . .]

Jakov: I am sorry to have lost my parents, but I know that I am with the Gospa. The Gospa has helped me very much to understand. I think that God desired them more than I.

Zorza: Did the Gospa guarantee you that your mother was with her?

Jakov: Yes.

Zorza: In Paradise, are the people all alike, or rather. . .?

Jakov: [. . .] No, they were not all alike.

INTERVIEW OF MIRJANA DRAGICEVIC
by Dom Pietro Zorza, transcribed by A. Bonifacio (excerpt)
(April 16, 1990)

(We have kept for these pages of interview, what Mirjana has not said in preceding interviews.)

Zorza: What is your greatest concern in communicating the messages?

Mirjana: The unbelievers, because the Gospa is always sad on the second of each month when she and I pray for them. She always speaks of them [. . .].

Zorza: When did you meet the Gospa for the last time?

Mirjana: On April 2. She spoke to me about unbelievers. On March 18, we had spoken about the Holy Mass.

Zorza: Will the secrets be revealed one by one or all at the same time?

Mirjana: One at a time.

Zorza: Tomislav [Vlasic] has said that the secrets are linked like a chain?

Mirjana: No, no. Many speak of that, but I cannot say anything: neither yes, or no, or how. I can only say that we must pray, nothing else [...].

Zorza: Can the secrets which have been entrusted to you change?

Mirjana: No. When the Gospa gave me the seventh secret, a part of this secret had concerned me very much. That is why I asked her if it could be changed. [...] We prayed very much and afterwards, once when she came, she told me that that part [of the seventh secret] was changed but that it was no longer possible to change the secrets, at least those which I received. [...]

Zorza: The secrets do not speak of good things. And yet you were married, Ivanka also. [...] Then that means that you hope? [...]

Mirjana: Yes, Ivanka and I believe very much in God and we are sure that God does not do anything bad. Do you understand? We have placed everything in the hands of God. That is all, and I cannot say anything else. [...]

Zorza: Have you seen Paradise?

Mirjana: For only two or three seconds, I have seen Paradise and Purgatory.

Zorza: And Hell?

Mirjana: No, I have not seen it, only Purgatory and Paradise and only for two to three seconds. It was like an apparition. The Gospa wants us to know that they exist because many say that there is no Purgatory, no Hell, and no Paradise.

Zorza: Have you seen the devil?

Mirjana: I do not want to speak about that.

Zorza: What impression do you have of Paradise?

Mirjana: There are the faces of people. One sees that they all have a light, a joy; we see that they are happy. That touched me very much. When I close my eyes, I always see again how happy they are. One does not see that on earth. They have another countenance. In Purgatory, I saw everything white as in the sands of Arabia.

Zorza: As in the desert?

Mirjana: Yes, I saw that people suffered something physically. I saw that they suffered, but I did not see why they suffered.

Zorza: Are the people in Paradise young, or very old, or children?

Mirjana: I said that I saw only for two or three seconds. The people that I saw were approximately 30 or 35 years old, but I saw very little.

Zorza: And the apparition? Up until now, you are, among the visionaries, the one who has described her the best.

Mirjana: It is not easy to describe what the Gospa is like. You can say that she is beautiful, but she is more than beautiful. Everything that you can say of her, she is even more because she has a beauty which cannot be described. One cannot just say that her eyes are blue or that her hair is long and black. This is so, but it is entirely something else. What she has, one cannot explain because she has love for everyone; she has a happiness, a light about her countenance that one cannot explain. Many times I tried to design (or paint) her countenance, but it is impossible.

Zorza: Speak to us of your meeting of April 2 [1990] with the Gospa; you said a locution.

Mirjana: We prayed several hours together for unbelievers. Every second of the month, up to then, she came at 11 in the evening until 3 or 4 in the morning. But on April 2, she came at 2:45 in the afternoon and stayed until 6:15. It is the first time that she came in the afternoon. I was alone at home and I experienced the same symptoms as in the evening when she comes. I felt a sweat was coming over me; I was nervous; I wanted to pray. And when I began to pray, I immediately felt that she was also praying with me. We did not speak about anything. We only prayed for unbelievers.

Zorza: Have you seen her?

Mirjana: This time, I only heard her.

Zorza: You told me once, that with the Gospa you pray as no one on earth has ever prayed.

Mirjana: Let us see! They are the normal prayers. We pray normally, but these prayers which we do are not the Rosary, not the "Our Father" or the "Hail Mary." It is another prayer which she has taught me and which I began to pray with her.

Zorza: May we know something about these prayers?

Mirjana: Once Vicka and I asked her how she spent her life. And she told us like a book. We wrote like a book the whole life of Our Lady. And in this book there are also prayers. In order to disseminate them, it is necessary to have first of all the permission to publish this book with the prayers which are found therein. Prior to that I cannot speak of anything. [. . .]

Zorza: Are sacrifice and fasting the two most powerful means to help prayer or rather does prayer suffice?

Mirjana: The two go together for me, because prayer is a beautiful thing, but fasting is a small thing which we can offer to God. It is a little cross which our body makes for God. [. . .]

Zorza: Should we pray for the souls in Purgatory?

Mirjana: Yes. When the Gospa said to pray for the unbelievers, she entrusted this task to me, while the souls in Purgatory, she entrusted them to Ivanka. In this way, to each visionary she entrusted something else. She told Ivan to pray for the youth. To answer your question, of course, to pray for the souls in Purgatory is very important. [. . .]

Now we pray together; during Lent we prayed a little more, [. . .] Wednesday and Friday we fast like all Christians who believe in God.

HOW DID MARIA LIVE THE FIRST APPARITION?
Her Recorded Testimony
(June 28, 1981)

Three days after the first apparition (June 25), Maria was asked by Fr. Jozo concerning the circumstances and the experience of this first apparition. Her testimony follows:

My sister had narrated to me the distant apparition she had seen on June 24. I listened, but I could not believe it. I said to her, "Ah, if I could see!"

For I already had the desire to see the Gospa. What is she like? We see her on images, but to be with her! (Vicka and the others were at my home and were preparing to leave in order to see whether by chance she would appear again along the way at the foot of the hill). I was anxious to go with them, but I told them, "I have something to do. You go on! If it happens, come and get me!"

Vicka said, "I will do it." A little later, I forgot all about it. Vicka then came running and said to me, "Come!" I answered her, "Okay, but where are we going?" She said, "Up there. Come!"

In front of our house, there was row of shoes. I took the first pair. I lost a shoe at the last house of the village, then another one at 20 or 25 meters farther down. It stayed there. I joined the others [barefooted], but I did not see her as they did. They were saying, "There she is!" But I did not see her on the hill. I said, "Let us go up there (to try to see)!" And they answered me, "Let us wait a little in order to see whether she is going to stay there." When I reached the top, she was not there. I did not see her. I asked myself: But what is it?

I stayed there at the site. The others arrived. They got on their knees and made the sign of the cross. I too made the sign of the cross like they did, but perhaps a little afterward. Then I saw her, and I fell on my knees. We all returned together. I told how she was gracious and beautiful [. . .]. I still saw her as if enveloped in a mist. Then she seemed to be clearer and clearer. At first I saw the form of her countenance and the rose-colored cheeks [...]. It is this rose color which I perceived before anything else. And I gradually saw all of her. She wore a white veil [...] and a long robe. How can one say? I do no know: I cannot describe it to you: like gray, but it is not gray. Brown colored? But it is not that either [...]. I do not have any idea. I do not know what that color is. The first time I did not hear her at all [...]. On Thursday [June 25], the others repeated to me what she said [...]. On Friday I heard her. She responded to all my questions. [Ivanka] asked, "How is my mother?" She answered, "Well [...]."

On the morning after, it was Mirjana who asked if she would return. She made a sign with her head [...] to say yes, that she would return.

Chapter 10

DOCUMENTS

Number 1

FR. UMBERTO LONCAR'S DIARY (FOUND IN CERIN, IN HIS PRESBYTERY NEAR MEDJUGORJE)

(May 28, 1990)

His diary is a valuable witness of the apparitions.

July 2, 1981: The police officers of the SUP, from Citluk, took the visionaries with them before the time for the apparitions. They say that they were mistreated with curses. The police officers insulted God, the Gospa, as well as their fathers and mothers ("swine"). They threatened to take them to the police in Sarajevo. They showed them their revolvers while warning them that it was not a simple ornament on their belts.

Friday, July 3, 1981: I left for Medjugorje in the morning. They told me that policemen occupied the parish house in Medjugorje until past midnight. They demanded that all the events be hushed up.

About 10:30, Bishop Zanic came to Citluk and questioned concerning the events in Medjugorje. We, the priests from Brotnjo, were gathered around the Bishop in the parish house at Citluk. We spoke about everything that had happened during the preceding days.

Finally the Bishop told us that the conversation of the children with the Gospa should be recorded on a tape recorder and that we should be prudent.

In the afternoon, about 6 o'clock, I arrived in Medjugorje. They were praying the Rosary in church, and after the Rosary they celebrated Mass. Enormous crowds were present in Medjugorje. Some went to the Hill of the Apparitions, others to the church.

The people did not know where the visionaries were or where the apparition would take place. I myself did not know where the children were.

At 6:15 p.m., I went from the church to the presbytery. I met Fr. Tadija Pavlovic. We asked a sister whether she knew where the children were. She showed us a room of the presbytery and told us: They are there!

We knocked at the door and entered. In the room were the children, Stojan Zrno, Mijo Gabric, Ivo Magzan, a young girl (relative of one of the visionaries), Fr. Todija Pavlovic, and myself. There were only four visionaries: Ivanka, Maria, and Jakov [the fourth was Ivan or Mirjana, according to a letter of Loncar on October 25, 1989]. Ivo Magzan looked at his wristwatch and told the children: "Pray, it is the hour of the apparition." The children seemed ill at ease and perplexed.

The young girl dressed in black [the visionary Ivanka Ivankovic] asked us to leave the room and to leave them alone because they were going to ask the Gospa that evening some things of a private nature. We answered that we did not understand anything of their conversation with the Gospa, but that if it were necessary to keep it secret, we promised absolutely to keep it. The children seemed to me very uneasy and scared. They were undoubtedly under the effects of the brutal acts of the day before. They resembled scared chicks which hide before the hawks. Anyway, Maria said, "Let us pray. It is the hour of the apparition."

Then the children began to pray and to sing. At 6:25 p.m. the Gospa appeared to them. The children fell on their knees. They stared fixedly at a point and moved their lips. We knelt down while observing them attentively. We did not see the Gospa or hear whatever was said. Little Jakov began to say something to the Gospa One could see his lips move. Then one of the children said in a loud voice: "Ode" [She is gone].

Immediately afterwards, Ivanka said loudly to Jakov, "Why did you ask that?" Then the children continued to pray and to sing. At 6:35 p.m. the Gospa appeared to them again. The conversation with her lasted two to three minutes. After that, we questioned them in order to know whether they could answer us: "Why did Ivanka tell Jakov 'Why did you say that?' " Ivanka answered that Jakov asked for a sign; then the children left immediately for the church.

I remained with Dom Tadija at the parish house. From there, one heard through the loud speakers that the children were telling the people in the church a message.

Immediately I was informed by some people concerning what the children had said. I note below their statements:

1. Little Jakov said:
   —The Gospa really appears to us. This evening also she appeared to us! It is a fact. I swear it on my life. I asked for a sign. And she lowered her head as if she approved. Then she disappeared.

2. Vicka said:
   —The Gospa appeared to us several times. This evening she gave messages for us and not for the world. When she appeared for the last time this evening, she said: "My angels, my angels! I bless you, you will be happy, and you will go into the bosom of your Father. Keep your faith."
   Then Vicka added:
   —Go in peace, goodbye to everyone!

After this testimony from Jakov and that of Vicka, there was loud applause in the church.

Number 2

NEW MEMORANDUM FROM MONSIGNOR ZANIC
(The Truth About Medjugorje)

At the beginning of March 1990, Msgr. Zanic released, for the third time, to the press and the episcopacy of the whole world, an unofficial memorandum against the apparitions which he entitled: *The Truth About Medjugorje.* This text was disseminated with 10,000 copies in Italian, 10,000 in English, 10,000 in German, and a larger number in Croatian. Msgr. Zanic did not publish a French translation, seeing the small audience that Medjugorje has in France. But two different translations have been made from the English version by supporters of Msgr. Zanic: *La Contra Reforme Catholique,* June 1990, and Mr. and Mrs. Cabaub, from Caju, who have widely disseminated their translation in the French press. The document is an important piece for the polemic file. I wanted to reproduce it here in my book, without commentary, but numerous readers concerned with the information, insisted that someone should help them sort out between the inaccuracies and the truth which Msgr. Zanic wants so nobly to promote. It is for these intentions, that notes have been published at the end of this document.

The discernment of the apparitions is a domain widely open to freedom of opinion in the Church, because it is not a dogma, and a Catholic who would have serious reasons about it has a right to challenge the apparitions, even apparitions recognized (as Fr. Dhanis, Rector of the Pontifical Gregorian University, did for Fatima). All the more reason, Msgr. Zanic maintains his freedom of expression with his particular authority, and, more modestly, those whom the grace of God has led to perceive the authenticity. It is within this spirit of openness, of freedom, and of communication in the service of truth, that we present his text and these notes, for the discernment of each one of us.

The document consists of 29 numbered articles.

Publisher's Note:
Father Laurentin's comments to these articles are indicated by footnote numbers, and these footnotes begin on page 201.

THE TRUTH ABOUT MEDJUGORJE
Unofficial Document of Msgr. Zanic

1. The truth about Medjugorje has been examined by the Yugoslav Episcopal Conference (BKJ). But their labors develop very slowly. Through the present writing, I wish to aid the Commission to arrive more quickly at a final judgment. The propaganda for Medjugorje hastens to put the Church and the world before the accomplished fact. It was the goal of the defenders of Medjugorje from the beginning. One must recognize that they have succeeded because the adversaries either work very slowly, or they are keeping silence. For this reason, and also by the requests of those who want to see the truth trampled, I decided, according to my responsibility and my conscience, to speak again and to help the Commission.

I wish to touch and awaken the conscience of those who defend Medjugorje. Their path is easy, wide and descending, while mine is steep, thorny, and ascending. The Church and the Gospa need only the truth. "The truth will make you free." (*Jn.* 8:32). "I am the Way, the Truth, the Life." (*Jn.* 14:6). "I have come to the world to give testimony to the truth. Whoever is of the truth, listens to My voice." (*Jn.* 18:37). Thus spoke Jesus.

To briefly summarize the lies of Medjugorje, it would be necessary to write at least 200 pages. For the moment, I limit myself to this brief writing without any scientific display. I am sorry to have to go so briefly to the front line, but since the beginning of the apparitions, I have found myself, from my function as bishop, in the center of the events. It displeases me also to have to report some "unpleasant things," but without it important arguments remain misunderstood.

2. The guide of the Atlas Agency of Dubrovnik, Marina B., sent to me in August 1989, a priest from Panama, Rodriguez Teofilo, parish priest of Our Lady of Lourdes. With him came the journalist Carmen Cecilia Caprilez, general manager of the Air Transport Agency, Panama. Marina introduced herself as guide, interpreter for the English language, and a convert of Medjugorje. The priest asked me why I did not believe in the apparitions. I answered him, "There are at least 20 reasons among which, one alone is sufficient, so that whoever is sound of spirit and instructed in the faith concludes that the apparitions are not supernatural."

He asked me to state at least one of these reasons. I briefly narrated to him the case of ex-priest Ivica Vego. For disobedience to the order from the Holy Father in 1982, he was expelled by the supreme authority of the Franciscan Order, released from his vows, and suspended *a divinis* [prohibition from exercising his functions as a priest]. He did not obey it. He continued to say Mass, to distribute the sacraments, and to visit his mistress. I hardly had to write it, but it is necesary in order to see about whom the Blessed Virgin speaks at Medjugorje. According to Vicka's diary and according to everything that the visionaries have said, the Gospa said at least 13 times that Vego is innocent but that the bishop is guilty. When his mistress, Sister Leopolda, a nun, became pregnant, both of them left Medjugorje and the religious life, married and they settled near Medjugorje where in the meantime another child was born.[1]

His prayer book continues to be sold in Medjugorje by thousands of copies.[2] I asked Marina, the guide, to translate it into English. It was not Marina's fault if she found herself in an environment which was hiding the truth. She reasoned spontaneously and sincerely according to her custom.

—My God, we will not reveal these unpleasant things (she said).

I answered her:

—If you had not kept hidden these "unpleasant things," the people of Panama would have known them and would not have come in vain to Medjugorje. It is dishonest and culpable to hide such truth although it may be painful. One has to say it.

3. Very similar is the behavior of Laurentin. He came to my house at Christmas 1983. I offered him dinner. He asked me why I did not believe in these apparitions. I answered him that the so-called Gospa, according to the diary of Vicka and the words of other visionaries, was against the bishop. He interrupted me point-blank:

—Do not publish it because there are many pilgrims and converts.[3]

The warning from this renowned mariologist shocked me. Nevertheless, such has remained the position of Laurentin up to this day: hide the truth, defend the lie. He has written tens of books, long and short, on Medjugorje, while almost always taking as his target Bishop Zanic and the truth. He knows well what pleases the ears of people and thus finds it easy to find someone who believes him: "Some will turn away from the truth, and they will turn toward fables." [*2 Tim.* 4:1]. The visionaries and the supporters of Medjugorje, led by Laurentin, have understood from the beginning that the modern believer in the communist state believes in everything that is strange, miraculous, in the so-called miraculous cures, in the so-called messages of the Madonna.

4. The principal rising columns in Medjugorje are Archbishop Franic and Laurentin, then L. Rupcic, Faricy S. J., Amorth, Rastrelli S. J., some Franciscans, and the charismatics of the whole world. In no time, they have published a number of books, articles, opuscules, produced films and video cassettes. [Thus there arose] travel agencies, pilgrimages, prayer books written by two Franciscans who had been expelled from the Franciscan Order: Vego and Ivan Prusina: 600,000 copies,[4] translated into all the languages of the world, prayer groups which became fanatics through the so-called messages of the Madonna, and the great motive of all that: money. No one mentions what casts a shadow over the apparition. The bishop is on watch. But the mechanism effaces everything.

They have spoken of 50 miraculous cures, of 150, 200, 300, etc.,[5] Laurentin has chosen 56 files sent to the Medical Bureau of Lourdes. Dr. Mangiapan answered him in the bulletin of April 1984, that this file had practically no value and could not be used or considered as a serious argument in favor of the apparitions of Medjugorje. One has written very much about the cure of Diana Basile. I sent the file to Lourdes. Dr. Mangiapan studied the case and stated a "more than reserved" opinion. It is a matter of multiple sclerosis.

5. The truth of the visionaries.
Mirjana Dragicevic: A month after the beginning of the apparitions, I went to Medjugorje to question the visionaries. I made all of them swear on the Cross, to say the truth, and that has been recorded. The first was Mirjana:
—We went to look for the sheep and all of a sudden . . . (but the vicar of the parish [Zrinko Cuvalo] had told me that they had gone to smoke while hiding from their parents).
—Be careful, Mirjana, I said to her, you are under oath. Did you go to look for the sheep? She put her hand to her mouth.
—Pardon me, we went to smoke.[6]

She also let me see her watch on which a miraculous thing had occurred. The hands were reversed. I took the watch and took it to the watchmaker. He said that the watch had been dropped and that it was out of order. I gave her back her watch and I suggested to her not to tell anyone that a miracle had taken place. On the eight cassettes which were made later, she continues to speak of the miracle of the watch, and to say that they had gone to look for the sheep.[7] Later, the Gospa stated that all religions are equal. To what extent may one believe what Mirjana said?[8]

6. *Vicka Ivankovic* is the main visionary of the first years and through her, Fr. Tomislav Vlasic, author from Medjugorje, issued the principal lies about Medjugorje. To the Pope, in a letter of April 13, 1984, he introduced himself thus: "I am Fr. Tomislav and it is I, according to Divine Providence, who guides the visionaries in Medjugorje."

It would have been better for him if he had retired to the desert and remained silent because his past says a lot about him. Vicka wrote very much and spoke very much. She also fell into many contradictions. A member of the first commission, a professor Bulat, questioned her and has written a 60-page study where he summarizes all the incoherences and lies of her diary.[9]

Here I would like to recall the bloody handkerchief. She stated that a taxi driver had met a man all bloody. This man gave him a handkerchief full of blood and told him:
–Throw it into the river.

He left and on the way he met a woman in black. She stopped him and asked him to give her a handkerchief. He gave her his, but she said to him:
—No, not that, but the one which is bloody!

He gave it to her, and she said to him:
—If you had thrown it into the river at that moment, it would have been the end of the world.

We asked the Gospa [Vicka writes in her diary] if it were true and she answered, "Yes," while adding:
—This bloody man was my Son, Jesus, and the woman in black was I [the Gospa].[10]

What kind of theology is that? Jesus wants to make the world perish while throwing a bloody handkerchief into the river, and the Gospa is the one that saves the world.

7. On January 14, 1982, Vicka, Maria and little Jakov came to my house. Vicka, deeply moved because she had not said the truth [told me]:

—The Gospa told us to tell you that in the remarks with the priests, you have acted precipitously.

—In what?

They answered: We do not know.

Fr. Vego and Fr. Prusina, chaplains in Mostar, whom the bishop made to leave Mostar because of their disorders and disobedience concerning the faithful belonging to the cathedral parish, which had been newly established, defended themselves before their superiors. They did not want to leave Mostar because the Gospa had told them through Vicka not to leave, to stay in Mostar as a member of the provincial government. I asked Vicka:

—Did the Gospa tell you anything about Vego and Prusina, the chaplains from Mostar?

—No, we do not know them, all three declared.

The conversation lasted a half hour. I recorded everything; I repeated several times the question concerning Vego and Prusina. But they "did not know them," they said. I will learn after that, from Vicka's diary, that they knew them very well. Since then, it was clear that they were telling lies. But I did not want to tell them in order to maintain confidence in our dialogues.[11]

8. On April 13, 1982, Vicka and Jakov, "sent by the Gospa" came to my house. The chaplains of Mostar, Vego and Prusina, had been driven out from the Order on January 20, by the supreme authority of the Franciscans. The supporters of Medjugorje and the Gospa fought for them. Vicka, very troubled, said:

—When we came to your house last time, we did not say to you what the Madonna had ordered. She reproached us about it and we, in the heat of the conversation, forgot it.

—What did you forget?

—The Gospa told us that Fathers Vego and Prusina are priests and they can also say Mass like other priests.

—Wait, wait, the Gospa told you that before you came to me last time?

—Yes, that is why she sent us to you. And I spoke of so many things that I forgot to tell you.

—Ah! But I asked you several times if the Gospa had told you something about the chaplains. . .

To me it was clear that she was lying, and it was for me proof that it was not necessary to trust them for the rest also. Maria and little Jakov took part in this lie.[12]

9. At the end of January 1983, Fr. Grafenauer, S. J., came to me with the intention of examining the phenomenon of Medjugorje. He listened to some 20 cassettes, and said that he would not go to Medjugorje because the Gospa was not there. On my suggestion, he went there and a few days later he returned, converted by Fr. Vlasic. He brought me some pages, put them on the table, and told me:

—That, Bishop, is what the Gospa tells you!

I became aware that it was a matter of a premeditated action: make the bishop fall with the help of the Gospa! These texts were a mixture of Vicka's diary, the parish chronicle, and transcriptions, so that it was difficult to establish authenticity of the original text. Vicka and the supporters of Medjugorje hid it from the bishop for more than a year. Here are some excerpts:

December 19, 1982: The Gospa said that for the confusion in Herzegovina, the most culpable was Bishop Zanic. As for Fr. Ivica Vego, she said that he was not guilty and that the bishop held all the power. She told him (Fr. Vego) to stay in Mostar and not to go away.

January 3, 1982: All the visionaries were questioned concerning Fr. Vego. The Gospa answered: Ivica is not guilty. If one expels him from the Franciscan Order, let him be courageous. . ."Ivica is not guilty." She repeated it three times.

January 11, 1982: We asked again concerning the two chaplains of Mostar, and the Gospa repeated twice what she had already said previously and on January 14, 1982. Vicka had been at the house of the bishop and said that she did not know Vego.

January 20, 1982: The children asked what Fr. Vego and Fr. Prusina were going to do if they were expelled from the Order. The Gospa answered:

—They are not guilty. The bishop has made a precipitous decision. Let them stay.

April 15, 1982: Vicka asked the Gospa:

—Tell me everything about Ivica Vego and Ivan Prusina.

The Gospa answered and said:
—They are not guilty.

She repeated it twice...
—The bishop made a mistake...Let them not leave Mostar; they can say Mass sometimes, but they may not move ahead so that everything may calm down. There is no fault in them.

April 16, 1982: Yesterday, while we were with the Gospa, we asked her if we could recite an "Our Father" for the two (Franciscan priests who had been punished). But she said immediately: "Yes." And she began to pray. When we finished, she smiled and said to me:
—You do not think about anything else other than those two!

I answered her: Yes, that is the way it is.

April 26, 1982: The Gospa [would have said]:
—The bishop does not have love for the true God. May Ivica and Ivan remain calm in what regards the bishop. What the bishop is doing is not according to the word of God. He can do what he wants, but one day we will see the justice which you have not seen for a long time.

10. Vicka never lied that the Gospa had told her that or that she wrote it. The certainty and authenticity of all this is confirmed in the best way by the cassettes which Fr. Grafenauer recorded with Vicka and Maria. He left a copy at the parish of Medjugorje, another one for the bishop, and another one for the Episcopal Conference in Zagreb. It is necessary to listen to it:

Conversation between Grafenauer and Vicka:
Grafenauer: The bishop is competent to judge if it is a matter of the Gospa or not.
Vicka: He can judge, but I know that it is the Gospa.
Grafenauer: The Church says that those who are sure of themselves prove that it is not a matter of the Gospa.
Vicka: Those who have this doubt have the right over it, but not I.
Grafenauer: This is not a good sign...You once told the bishop that he had to listen to the Gospa rather than the Pope.
Vicka: Yes, I said it.

Grafenauer: That means that the bishop should listen to you, you more than the Pope.

Vicka: No, not me.

Grafenauer: And the bishop does not know what it is. Perhaps it is not the Gospa.

Vicka: The Gospa! The Gospa!

Grafenauer: You have told the bishop that he is to blame and that those two (Vego and Prusina) are not to blame and that they can continue to exercise their priestly functions.

Vicka: Yes, I said it.

Grafenauer: Can they hear confessions? Did the Gospa say it?

Vicka: Yes.

Grafenauer: If the Gospa says it and the Pope says no?

Vicka: The Pope can say it, but I said things the way they are.

Grafenauer: That will conclude: it is not the Gospa. When the Pope says: "They cannot celebrate Mass, they cannot hear confessions" and the Gospa says: "Let them hear confessions, let them celebrate," it is unacceptable.

Vicka: I know what is true (as the Gospa said it).

Grafenauer: If the Gospa said so, I would put my hand in the fire that it was not the Gospa. The more a man receives great gifts, the more there is the danger that the devil is involved in it

What shame and offense for the Gospa! That is how the Gospa would destroy obedience in the Church: obedience to the bishop, the government of the Franciscans, to the Holy Father. She defends Vego![13]

THE APPARITION IN CERNO

11. The apparition is a neighboring place of Medjugorje. The week after the beginning of the apparitions, there was an apparition in Cerno. What "happened"—the visionaries narrated it the same evening to the Curé, Fr. Jozo Zovko. They said that the Gospa had said four or five times that she would still appear for three days, that is to say, July 1, 2 and 3: Wednesday, Thursday, and Friday. It was recorded then published by Fr. Ivo Sivric. The cassette was reproduced in numerous copies. Several years later, Fr. Janko Bubalo published the book: *A Thousand Encounters with the Gospa*. They are conversations with Vicka. Seeing that she does not recall this fact, Fr. Janko asked her if the Gospa had said "three more days." She answered that she did not remember.

It is obvious that Vicka did not say the truth and that the Gospa cannot say what Vicka narrates. Vicka invents. Can that remain hidden from the world? One cannot do badly (say lies about the Gospa) in order to obtain good (pilgrimages, prayer...).

THE VISIONARY MARIA PAVLOVIC

12. Here we transcribe the conversation recorded by Fr. Grafenauer:

Grafenauer: Did the Gospa say that the bishop was guilty?
Maria: Yes.
Grafenauer: Did she say that Vego and Prusina were not guilty?
Maria: Yes.
Grafenauer: If the Gospa says that the bishop is guilty, one begins immediately to doubt that it is about the Gospa...And then the visionaries spread the news that the bishop is guilty.
Maria: The Gospa told us that.
Grafenauer: That created the revolt in Herzegovina, and these are not good fruits. The people are going to get angry against the bishop and denigrate him. How could the Gospa do a similar thing? The Church knows that the Gospa is good and that she would not do such things.
Maria: The Gospa spoke to us in this way.

Archbishop Franic, R. Laurentin, and many others know that, but they keep silent. What kind of theology is that which accepts that the Gospa proclaims to her children and through them to the whole world that their master, pastor, and priest, to whom Christ through the Church has legitimately entrusted the Church, the bishop does not have the least love of God in him and thus, declares him a public sinner before the whole world, and invites him to conversion? And in Medjugorje they will pray for such an intention. They have also affirmed that Jesus will pray for him so that he may believe and act more decisively in favor of the events in Medjugorje. To say that the Gospa's judgment touches the bishop is an absurd thing, an offense to the Gospa, Mother of the Church. I am not without sin, and the Lord can find to reproach me. But the Lord is the only judge for my episcopal ministry; I have never been reprimanded by the Holy See.[14]

13. Fr. Tomislav Vlasic has printed and disseminated among other things 17 pages in the principal languages [untitled]: *An Appeal During the Marian Year*, Milan, March 25, 1988. It is about the foundation and the call to a new community of prayer of young people (from Medjugorje) in a community life at Parma (Italy). It is an unheard of fact in the history of the Church. They are supposedly to save the world. The inspirations and initiatives have been given to him and to a German, Agnes Heupel, supposedly cured in Medjugorje. And with Vlasic, she directed the community, like [Saint] Francis and [Saint] Clare, said Vlasic. So that the undertaking could succeed, the visionary Maria, on the request of Tomislav Vlasic, added three pages: *My Testimony*. She is a member of the community and writes on April 21, 1988:

"I also feel the need to say some words concerning the information written by Fr. Tomislav...As you see, the Gospa gave a program for the community, Queen of Peace [. . .], and led this community through Fr. Tomislav and Agnes, through whom the messages for the community come. I have been in the community for more than a month and a half.

"I have apparitions and the Gospa introduces me into the mystery of love and of suffering which is the basis of this community. I must write everything and I will make it public when the Gospa will tell me." (p. 15-16 from Fr. T. Vlasic).

The supporters of Medjugorje quickly understood that the community of boys and girls established in the house for life, prayer, work, sleep, will destroy itself and also Medjugorje and they sent their provincial, Fr. Jozo Vasilj, to Parma. The latter took with him Bishop Benito Cocchi and Fr. Tomislav Vlasic and led them to the Congregation in Rome. And there, they told him that the Church cannot approve it, and they notified Tomislav Vlasic to dissolve the community and to return to Herzegovina. Vlasic did not obey immediately and his return took place later. Fr. Jozo Vasilj thus presented it to me.

14. On July 11, 1986, the same Maria Pavlovic[15] made another public statement of one page concerning the Vlasic text:

"I feel the moral obligation to say what follows before God, the Madonna, and the Church of Jesus Christ.

"From the text, *An Appeal,* it appears that I have brought an answer from the Gospa to a request of Fr. Tomislav Vlasic.

"Now I state that I never asked the Gospa for any confirmation, whatever it be, concerning the work of Tomislav and Agnes Heupel. My first testimony, such as was published in the Croatian and Italian languages, does not correspond to the truth. Fr. Tomislav advised me several times (sic), to write as a visionary, a testimony awaited by the world...

"All that which can be understood as an answer and explicit confirmation of the work of Tomislav Vlasic and Agnes Heupel on the part of the Gospa through me does not correspond to the truth at all...I sign this statement before the Most Blessed Sacrament."

15. Maria does not deny having given the first statement. Fr. T. Vlasic complained to her several times for this statement and that is called a manipulation of the visionary. We also affirm: Maria, consciously, either the first or the second time, did not say the truth. She said lies, and she attributes them to the Gospa. It is evident that she is a rattle in the hands of T. Vlasic. Not only now, but since the beginning. That was clear to me. But up to then, I did not have material proof in my hands. In this way then, Fr. Tomislav Vlasic manipulated all the visionaries. In this same way, Maria saw the Gospa cry when someone in the prayer group mentioned the bishop: "A large tear flowed from the Gospa's eyes. It came down on her countenance and disappeared in the cloud which was under her feet...The Gospa cried and she went up to Heaven while crying." (August 22, 1984). An invention of Tomislav Vlasic in order to scare the bishop.

Why do the supporters of Medjugorje not mention these two statements by Maria? What one must hide from the world are these unpleasant things, although in Medjugorje there are only conversions (Laurentin). Laurentin writes in his book that a prelate prayed to the Gospa to give a message for his priests. And Maria: "The Gospa said that they read the books of Laurentin about Medjugorje and that they disseminate them."

It is a horrible sin to attribute these very lies to the Gospa. When the world will know it, who will believe then? They will be discredited. No one can destroy this proof. They will be disseminated and copied. I know that there are many for whom all that means nothing because they see Medjugorje in an irrational and emotional way and in the point of view of their own interests. They are blind, but these documents will remain in the history of the Church and of mariology.

THE "VISIONARY" IVAN DRAGICEVIC

16. Vicka writes in her diaries, 13 times of the great sign; in the chronicle of the parish, 14 times; on the cassettes, 52 times; in the conversations with the bishop, numerous times. In the spring of 1982, I asked the visionaries to write everything concerning the (promised) great sign without revealing the secret. They had to write it in two copies, close their envelopes, one for them and the other for the bishop. When the sign would come, one would open the envelopes and one would see whether the sign had been predicted beforehand. The curé of the time, Fr. T. Vlasic, told the visionaries: —Say that the Gospa told you not to write anything for anyone.

And they did not write anything.

Ivan Dragicevic was in the Franciscan seminary of Visoko in Bosnia and did not know anything about it. Two members of the Commission, Drs. M. Zavic and Z. Puljic (today Bishop of Dubrovnik) went to his room. They gave him a light green paper and some type-written questions. Ivan wrote, without a word and without fear, the content of the sign with the date and his signature. Some years later, Laurentin wrote that Ivan had told he had not written anything and that he had circumvented the members of the Commission. Then, on March 7, 1985, three members of the Commission of Medjugorje went to his house to ask him if what Laurentin had written was true. He answered:

—Yes, and one can open the envelope which has been kept at the Chancery. Inside there is only white paper. They returned, and before the members of the Commission gathered in Mostar, they opened the letter. On the light green paper was written the sign: "The Gospa said that she would leave a sign. 'This sign, I say to you and I entrust to you, will be in Medjugorje a great sanctuary in honor of my apparitions and this sanctuary will be dedicated to me.'

—When?

—The sign will come in the month of June.

Date of the statement: May 9, 1982. Signed: Ivan Dragicevic."

In the presence of such an enormous lie, the members of the Commission wanted to interrupt all further examination. Nevertheless, they continued their work. Slavko Barbaric led the visionaries for some days and instructed them so that all, including Ivan, affirmed that Ivan had not revealed the sign (sic!).

Ivan sent to the bishop the messages which the Gospa had given him. Thus, on April 24, 1984, the Gospa spoke thus of the bishop:

"My son Jesus prays for him so that he can believe and become more involved with greater decision for the events in Medjugorje."

And still: "How would he react if my Son would come down to earth? Would he believe then?"

With respect to the Commission, the Gospa said only this: "Pray, pray, pray (sic). Meditate and live the messages and you will understand why I have come."

17. "Tell the bishop that I ask him urgently for his conversion to the events of the parish of Medjugorje before it is too late. Let him begin an approach to all the events with much comprehension, love, and with a great responsibility. I desire that he not create conflict among the priests and that he cease to put in relief the negative side.

"The Holy Father gave all the bishops the responsibility to fulfill certain functions in their respective dioceses and to resolve the problems and disputes. The bishop is the main priest of all the parishes in Herzegovina. He is the head of the Church in Herzegovina. For this reason, I ask him for conversion to the events. I send him a last warning.

"If he does not convert and does not correct himself, my judgment and the judgment of my Son will reach him. This will mean that he has not found the way to my Son Jesus." The Gospa told me to give you this message. (signed) With many greetings. Ivan Dragicevic, Biakovici, June 21, 1983."

This message was brought to me by Fr. Tomislav Vlasic and, according to all probability, it is he who composed it in a moment of exaltation.

18. Ivan has been writing his diary of the apparitions for several years. It has not been published any more than the diaries of Vicka or of all the others who wrote them. It is a matter of original sources, full of ingenuity, of lies, of truisms, and absurdities. They are a good proof that the visionaries do not see the Gospa and do not receive any message from her. These messages were composed by someone else and delivered to Ivan for his signature. When Fr. Grafenauer brought me the excerpts of Vicka's diary from Medjugorje, I asked him to bring me her diary. She wrote to me on May 7, 1983: "I have learned that someone is revealing excerpts from my diary. . ."

It is an important confession that this diary, Vicka wrote it and has regarded it as her own, and it has become a key argument in the hands of the Commission. Fr. T. Vlasic has accounted for it, and in 1984, he stated before me and before the Commission that this letter, it was not Vicka who wrote it, but a priest (probably he) and that it was sent to her for her signature (sic!). There are many manipulations of this kind, but one does not have any proof as for this one.[16]

19. Since the first days of the apparitions, the visionaries, evidently instructed to make control impossible, told everyone tht the Gospa spoke differently to each one of them. When the secrets were invented, each one had to have his own (thus 60 secrets!) and they must not be revealed to anyone.[17]

Mirjana and Ivanka received from the Gospa a special letter which no one can read![18]

At the beginning there was no ecstasy or disconnection with the others. One could speak to the visionaries and they could speak to the people. But they escaped from the Commission.

Having been instructed, as they have said so themselves, they asked the Gospa if they could write the great sign and leave it in a closed envelope, and the Gospa said no.

Ivan wrote it, then he said later (recorded on a tape recorder) that the Gospa did not reproach him for it.[19] The secrets will be delivered to a priest (a Franciscan); why not to the Commission or to the bishop or to the Holy Father? During the first months, they often said:

—until the great sign, little time, very soon, before long. When the first year passed, they changed their tone.

For a year and a half, Vicka wrote *"The Life of the Gospa"* and the great sign will be published "when the Gospa will permit it."

The Commission has asked for this diary, but the Gospa does not permit it. Can the Commission see it without taking it or opening it? No! It is a large stroke of inspiration to lead the ingenuous of the whole world by the tip of the nose, and they will wait for the secret and the great sign until the end of the world. I have already made it known and I repeat: if the Gospa leaves a sign of which the "visionaries" speak, I will go on my knees from Mostar to Medjugorje (30 kilometers) and I will ask the Franciscans and the visionaries to forgive me.[20]

20. "At the beginning, the bishop believed." Thus spoke some people. It is not true. When the Communists persecuted the priests, the visionaries, and the pilgrims, I defended them all, and I never changed my mind because the Commission of the Republic (of Bosnia-Herzegovina) had threatened, and because the (secular) priests demanded it of me. Those are calumnies: pure inventions, some among many.[21]

While I publicly defended the Franciscans in prison, Fr. Jozo Zovko said that his bishop, during the instruction [of his trial], is "a wolf and a hypocrite." It is in his act of accusation. His lawyer, Bukovic, asked me through a colleague what I had done to Jozo Zovko for him to accuse me so.[22]

Fr. Tomislav Vlasic often placed in the mouth of the visionaries the statements of the Gospa that Satan (the bishop, he insinuated) wants to destroy her plan, and about that he wrote more openly to his friends in the Vatican. I took him again before his provincial for having called the bishop, Satan. He did not deny my accusation, but he justified himself of having written those things in his "excitement" (sic!). One can say many things in excitement but not write them and translate them into foreign languages.[23]

21. The main argument of the supporters of Medjugorje is this. One sees by its fruits that the Gospa is appearing. Those who know more, on seeing the pilgrims who come to Medjugorje, say: By the fruits of the most involved heroes of Medjugorje, one sees that they do not believe in the apparitions [the Bishop seems to want to say that their fruits are profit and immorality]. And if one could say all these unpleasant things, naturally the negative would be clear to anyone. But Laurentin, Rupcic, Vlasic, Barbaric, and others carefully hide the truth.[24] If the supporters of Medjugorje meet someone who expresses personal doubts about the apparitions, they isolate him, persecute him, or say that he is crazy (J. L. Martin). The majority of the pious people allow themselves to be taken in by enormous propaganda, the fable of the apparitions, the miracles; and these enthusiasts and fanatics become the best propaganda. It does not come to them, even to the spirit, that the truth is hidden and that the message is brutally imposed upon them.

They do not even know that no miraculous cure is produced which is not examined by experts and competent institutions like the Medical Bureau of Lourdes. No one knows anything about the cures of Herzegovina. Little Daniel, old Jozo Vasilj, Venka Brajcic, and others mentioned in the first books about Medjugorje, everyone knows today that they were not cured.

22. The promises of cures are characteristic. When they are not achieved, one denies them because they have not been recorded or stated in writing. But many have ended in a tragic way. It is interesting to know if the promises are from the Gospa or, rather, an invention of the visionaries.

Very much has been said about the tragic end of Marko Blazvic, told by Msgr. Turk, Archbishop of Belgrade. He wrote on Mary 22, 1984, that he had become ill and admitted into the cardiology service of the hospital in Belgrade. He was assigned a bed next to Marko Blazvic. Marko told the archbishop what he had told other patients, nurses, and doctors: the Gospa had promised him through the intermediary of the visionaries that the operation would succeed assuredly. The sister who assisted at the operation wrote to me later that Marko's spouse and daughter told the same same thing with a faith near fanaticism in the promise of the Gospa. A doctor allowed himself to be convinced of the authenticity of this promise. The patient never recovered after the operation. During it, a group of people prayed with fervor before the door of the operating room, and many spoke of this incident which caused much disillusion and shame before the atheists and people of other religions. Fr. T. Vlasic, who had hidden the truth, succeeded in convincing the daughter of the deceased Marko, to go to the bishop to tell him that the Gospa had only spoken of praying, without promising the success of the operation. I told him not to bury the deceased father in lies and the others who heard what he was telling them.[25]

23. The relations between the Franciscan and diocesan clergies were regulated by a decision of the Holy See in 1899. On the recommendation of the Franciscans and the Franciscan bishop, Pascal Buconijic, the parishes had to be divided into two equal parts: 50 percent to the Franciscans and 50 percent to the diocesan clergy. For lack of diocesan priests, in 1923, the parishes were entrusted to the Franciscans *(ad nutum Sanctae Sedis)*.

In 1948, Msgr. Cule, first diocesan bishop of Mostar, was condemned to 11 years and 6 months in prison. He served 8 and a half years of his punishment before being released. After this time in prison, the diocesan clergy multiplied. In 1968, the Holy See ordered the Franciscans to give five parishes to the diocesan clergy. They gave only two in 1975, and after that the discussions lasted for years. Finally, a decree from the Holy See ordered the division of the parishes. The Franciscans rejected publicly and collectively this decree [restrictive], although they had in the diocese of Mostar 80 percent of the faithful to administer. In 1976, because of this disobedience to the Holy See, the hierarchy of the province, and Provincial Silic, were deprived of their authority. Since that time, the province and the general of the Order govern it *ad instar*. In 1979, another sanction was taken which prevented the Franciscans of Herzegovina from attending the general chapter for the election of the general. The first point of the first letter of the new general to his brothers was: the renewal of obedience and collaboration with the bishop in Herzegovina.

Today disobedience prevails, as in the past. And the Gospa from the beginning [of the apparitions] supports the Franciscans. Vicka wrote in her diary of the apparitions that, according to the Gospa, the bishop was responsible for the disorder in Herzegovina (see previous no. 9). This was repeated several times. The Franciscans are divided. The opposition which defends Medjugorje has succeeded in shaking their superior *ad instar* (= simili superior) who spoke of good relations with the bishop and installed the group which supports Medjugorje. The new provincial *ad instar*, Fr. Jozo Vasilj, did not succeed in establishing order and peace among his own. That is why he fled to the missions of Zaire. He will not return from them any more (Fruits!). He was replaced by a vice provincial while the general claims obedience from all and threatens to suppress the province. It is time for each one to accept his own responsibilities before juridical sanctions are taken or the province is suppressed (Acts of the Order, fasciculus I/89). The province will not receive its own hierarchy until the decree is executed. Three visitors of the Franciscan Order who came in 1988 say that there are no Franciscans in the province who are favorable to the execution of the decree. This warning is exaggerated and yet important.[26]

24. The pilgrims only know that "the bishop hates the Franciscans." Yet, there are a good number of Franciscans who collaborate with the bishop and do not believe in the apparitions. Some of them have never gone to Medjugorje.

A certain number of good Franciscans ask and beseech me to write something in order to begin together the battle against the lies of Medjugorje because "God will punish us severely, us Franciscans," for having filled the world with lies and errors and for having drawn material profit from it.

Of the 100 diocesan priests of Herzegovina, not a single one believes in the apparitions. Of the 42 bishops in Yugoslavia (ordinary, auxiliary, or retired), only one has stated publicly that he believes and he fights for Medjugorje.[27] Of the 15 members of the first Commission of Investigation established by the bishop with other bishops and provincials from Yugoslavia, 11 of them declared that there was nothing supernatural in the events in Medjugorje. Two [Franciscans] proclaimed the authenticity of the apparitions. A member said that there was something taking root at the beginning. And another abstained himself from voting.[28]

Concerning what the Commission has worked on in three years, contrary to what the defenders of Medjugorje have disseminated, the Holy See has never requested anything. It has not expressed any judgment over it and has not rejected the bishop.[29]

25. Since the beginning of these events, I warned the Franciscans so that they would not anticipate the judgment of the Church and collaborate in the search of the truth. But the leaders of these events had as their objective, to increase as quickly as possible, the crowds

in Medjugorje in order to accumulate much money for their propaganda and to take advantage of the Gospa for their struggle against the bishop. They invented the miracles of the sun. Pilgrims suffered serious lesions while looking at the sun. They spoke of 50, 250, 300 cures. They spoke without rhyme or reason, seeing that the people were ready to believe everything that they told them as long as everything was supported by Fr. Franic, Laurentin...Those who believe in Medjugorje look at the events as they present them, as in the case in other places of apparitions, be they true or false. The enthusiasm and the emotion have been deliberately driven up to absolute blindness and fanaticism.

26. The Italians know well the history of Gigliola Ebe Giogini, who established a pseudo-congregation: La Pia Opera of Merciful Jesus. A divorcee, later married by civil law, healer, she made charlatanism, recruited young girls for her congregation. She received very much money. She had two priests in her service and several houses. She had many jewels and gold, two yachts, 32 furs, etc. She led a double life. She had false stigmas which she made on herself. Her sisters followed her with fanaticism and called her Mama Ebe. She also had some male vocations. Some sisters left her and they told of her immoral life. Many in the Church condemned her. Fanatically defended by others, she claimed some "good fruits." She even obtained the praise of two bishops. Twice at night the police broke into the room of the mother house and surprised her in the act with a novice. The scandal exploded. She was condemned to several years in prison, and with her, a Franciscan, her confessor. The newspapers enjoyed themselves for several years with her scandals. They made a movie of her shame. And yet, her pupils followed her fanatically and defended her blindly even when her congregation had been dissolved. For them, she was a saint who gave rise to vocations. For many this was the decisive argument. As for fruits, one saw that she was a woman of God: vocations, vocations, cures, fruits, fruits. Religious blindness cures with difficulty. Fanaticism is at the beginning of heresy. Today it is the foundation of sects.

Reverend Jones, a Protestant pastor from Chicago, developed an enormous charitable activity and amassed large amounts of money and fanatic disciples for his sect. To be more free in their action, they went to South America, to Guyana. They founded a village, Jamestown, under the dictatorship and fanatical obedience to their messiah. People have written about these diverse and horrible things and about Jones' immorality. Some of his followers tried to flee but were killed. Then the money disappeared and they said that the American army was coming. Then Jones ordered everyone to withdraw into the jungle. Not seeing another way out, he invited all of them to transfer to the other world. Approximately 900 approached a basin with their glasses. They drank poison and died. What gave them the strength to die? Fanaticism. When one speaks to Christians of apparitions and miracles, they easily lose their critical sense through blindness and fanaticism. One believes everything that he says. They say that a simple rosary in Medjugorje changes into gold and one believes it.[30]

27. This blindness of Medjugorje reaches priests and some bishops.[31] Many priests from Italy: Amorth, Rastrelli, and others have easily been able to hear that the bishop, the Commission, the bishops of Yugoslavia, as well as a part of the priests and diocesan clergy, do not believe. But they have fled the truth, although I have graciously devoted to some of them very much of my time.

I am particularly surprised at the lack of collegiality of some bishops. No one has the obligation to accept my judgment, but each one has the responsibility to study the events of Medjugorje according to his conscience before taking a position, especially if he occupies in the Church a function such as that of bishop.

"My Gospa, what have they done with you?" For nine years they have dragged you about like a tourist attraction. They speak with you to their liking, as with one employed at the gate [of Heaven]. They report invented messages. They say that you come there and that you are appearing, but beginning with their own statements, they do not have any proof of what they say. They keep the whole world in expectation of the "great sign." The ingenuous believe and wait. And yet this false impression will bring great shame and scandal to the Church. The guides are not converted and over them all weighs the threat of their general to dissolve the [Franciscan] province. That is a small part of what I would want to write. I will treat it more amply in a documented book which I hope to be able to publish soon.

28. They say that in Medjugorje there is very much prayer, piety, conversions. I have indeed received many moving letters. I am sorry for those who, sooner or later, will suffer a disillusion. There is

still much fanaticism, superstition, and ignorance of the events of Medjugorje. I have also received letters filled with vulgar offenses which one cannot publish. And it is always in the name of the Queen of Peace.[32]

The positive can in no way justify lies in order to gain the world for God. "I came to the world to give testimony to the truth," said Jesus. (*Jn.* 18:37). Even today the Church could attract to it large masses if it abolished the sixth commandment of God and recognized divorce, if it left to each one the freedom to believe and to do what he wanted. And yet, Jesus went to the Cross for the truth. Martyrs gave their lives for the truth. St. Paul wrote to his faithful: "If someone preaches to you a gospel different from that which you received, let him be anathema." (*Gal.* 1:9).

Today many prayer groups throughout the world use the prayer book by Ivica Vego and meditate on the so-called messages of the Gospa as if it were more important than the Bible and the Magesterium of the Church. I think that the Gospa will obtain for the Church the grace to live the truth of Christ.

I know that there will be good and pious souls who will not understand me, to whom I will appear as the enemy of the Blessed Virgin. I have been many times to Lourdes and to other sanctuaries tied to apparitions recognized by the Church. I choose the truth. I defend the Holy Church; I pray to God to be able to sacrifice my life for it.

29. Those who have written books about Medjugorje have sold them very well and have become rich. Those, on the contrary, who have criticized have not been successful because they have met an organized boycott.[33]

In order to know the reverse of the coin, one must read: [the Bishop quotes here three books from opponents]: the Italian Gramaglia; Sivric, edited in Canada by L. Belanger, and the American M. Jones, [whose references one will find in the analysis in *Seven Years*, no. 7, and *Eight Years*, no. 8].

In further response to the above document by Bishop Zanic, further clarification is presented on the following pages regarding "cures" and the alledged "end of the apparitions."

FOOTNOTES

1. This paragraph no. 2 confuses the facts, the dates, and the plans. On reading it, one would think that Ivica Vego had been punished for misconduct, and that he published a book that is food for the pilgrims. But this book is not his (see the following note) and it was moreover published before his mistake. To read Msgr. Zanic, one would also think that the Gospa had approved his mistake for which he himself was sorry. The answers of the visionaries regarding Vego (1982-1984) are prior by more than two years to the failure recalled by Msgr. Zanic. Ivica Vego is a Franciscan from Mostar and not from Medjugorje, as this indictment would try to make one think. He was indicted *before* the apparitions. He was punished in 1982 for reasons completely foreign to Medjugorje: the conflict between Franciscans and seculars on the matter of the cathedral (which we gave details in *Messages and Teachings,* Annex 1). When Msgr. Zanic states that Fr. Ivica Vego and Sister Leopolda "left Medjugorje," he completely distorts the "truth" which he claims he wants to cultivate. Ivica Vego and Sister Leopolda did not live in Medjugorje, but in the bishop's city of Mostar at the provincial house of the Franciscans. It is then false to locate them in Medjugorje.

   With respect to Ivica Vego's fault, he was fervent and courageous in adversity for a long time. He wanted to keep his vow of chastity and the others in spite of the annulment with which he had been struck. He was ready to leave Mostar (since there would be a regular judgment), after it had been heard, and not a simple administrative sanction. He had succeeded in 1986 in having his case judged by the supreme court of the Church (the apostolic signature), and this judgment was stopped by a high administrative authority in Rome, in order not to cause trouble for those who had already taken the sanctions in a canonically deficient manner. This interference into the judiciary, and the low state in which he found himself after so many years, made him lose his head with the (very) compassionate sister Leopolda. He repented of his fault, but he preferred to accept the consequences (the woman and the child) rather than a solution of abortion or abandonment. Such is the truth, although Msgr. Zanic disguises it and delays in disclosing it.

2. The prayer book in question has as its author Slavko Barbaric, a Franciscan of great spiritual influence, and not Ivica Vego. If Vego's name appears in the first editions, it is by virtue of his editorial assistance and not as author.

3. Since 1984, Msgr. Zanic repeats this falsehood which I have continuously contradicted since the beginning. In spite of my repeated warnings, Msgr. Zanic brought it up again before French journalists which had gathered in his cathedral. I interrupted him to remind him of my contradiction. He had the good grace to stop there. I was grateful to him for it. Why does he take it up again now (with others as unjust) in more than 40,000 copies?

   In fact, I had invited him not to expose in public the sordid quarrels which afflicted his diocese. And especially, I had asked him not to publish inaccurate things and, in addition, defamatory, against his adversaries, which harms not only Medjugorje but his own reputation. It is the same feeling which the interpreter Marina expressed to him. He has invited her to spread the "unpleasant things."

4. The book, which is by Slavko Barbaric (and not by the two alleged priests, see note 2), has had great success. But the number of 600,000 copies seems excessive. We do not know on what it was based.

5. Msgr. Zanic speaks ironically with humor. The contradiction between the numbers would prove that there were no cures. But the figures are not contradictory. In 1983, Fr. Rupcic had prepared a summary inventory of 55 declared cures at the parish. But this number continued to increase since that time. There were 339 cures to March 1988, and 361 my next-to-last trip to Medjugorje (May 28, 1990). The work load at the place of pilgrimage, increases unceasingly, and the transfer of Fr. Ivan Dugandzic, who collected the documents with care and confidence, has hindered these archives. It would be desirable for a lay archivist or a medical office to be able to record henceforth these cures which continue. See pages 213-214 of this text regarding the cures in question.

6. After six years Msgr. Zanic again brings up this accusation of a lie. Mirjana did not lie but only remained silent over this minor

and embarrassing aspect of the walk of June 24. Msgr. Zanic, informed about this detail by the vicar of Medjugorje, Fr. Zrinko Cuvalo, questioned Mirjana (and Ivanka) on that, dramatically and under oath. And they recognized the fact immediately. They did not lie about it. And they did not lie on saying that they went to look for the sheep with Milka, which they indeed did, as Milka the shepherdess also verified.

7. The watch: This peculiarity of her watch amazed Mirjana, who had just requested "a sign" from the Gospa, but there is no lying or cheating. Only an exceptional, unexplained fact of which one cannot draw an argument either for or against.

8. Here again, Msgr. Zanic goes out of his context and distorts a statement from Mirjana. This problem is treated *ex professo* in *Messages and Teachings,* Appendix #2. One will find there the collection of texts and the interpretation according to the cultural milieu where the words have a particular meaning. When the visionaries speak of religion, they do not mean the doctrine at all, but the persons, so often hurt in the strained and passionate relations of which the Balkans suffer.

9. Fr. Nicolas Bulat (expert on the Commission of Msgr. Zanic), today deceased, in fact wrote a critical memorandum against Vicka. The Commission had not kept this scrupulous but unilateral analysis. Contrary to what the Bishop says, it is not Vicka, it is Mirjana who was the principal source of the letter to the Pope, as Tomislav says explicitly in his letter.

10. The bloody handkerchief: When I finished the French edition of Bubalo's book, I asked him to withdraw this mythical and badly founded account. He decided to keep it in. I respected his right of authorship and I have always made the most expressed reservations concerning this account, which came no one knows from where or how. It is necessary to place it in the agitation phase of Medjugorje, analogous to the agitation phase of Lourdes (May, 1858), about which I likewise made criticism in *Lourdes, documents authentiques,* volume 2.

11. Concerning this complicated matter, see R. Laurentin, *Messages and Teachings,* Appendix #1.

In her first conversation with the Bishop, Vicka had remained silent, diplomatically and through deference, about certain information as occurs in every conversation, even in the church. Nothing more. Msgr. Zanic confesses that he did the same: "I did not tell them in order to maintain their confidence." Vicka's omission had the same motif. Why should her silence be lies, and that of the bishop, virtuous prudence?

12. Ibid. See *Messages and Teachings,* Appendix #1, in order to place this point within the context.

13. Concerning the numbers 9 and 10, see likewise *Messages and Teachings,* Appendix #1, concerning the cited texts which are covered there in detail.

14. Far from remaining silent on this same issue, as Msgr. Zanic reproaches me, I have treated it in a very broad manner (Appendix 1 of *Messages and Teachings*). The bishop has been reprimanded by Rome.

    More, Fr. Grafenauer, expert in discernment with whom Msgr. Zanic had consulted about Medjugorje, has finished with a favorable conclusion, much to the regret of the bishop who has dismissed him as a result. Since that time, Fr. Grafenauer does not cease to protest against the use which is made of his testimony, contrary to the facts and conclusions which he has established (see notably *Latest News*). He has also expressed his confusion concerning the use made of his name and of his documentation in numbers 10 and 12 of this document edited here. Following the memorandum of Msgr. Zanic, he sent to the Commission of Investigation, a statement on the matter which he does not wish to reveal.

15. Maria's break with the community of Fr. Tomislav Vlasic: We have discussed this matter in *Eight Years.*

    The difference of opinion of Maria concerning the orientation of the community of Tomislav Vlasic when she entered, and concerning the position which T. Vlasic gave to the oracles of Agnes Heupel, are an incident as often happens in communities in the process of founding a new model. This disagreement does not concern in any way the apparitions and their authenticity.

16. Ivan's faux pas, called on to write the sign (no. 16-18). In summary, Ivan, separated from the other visionaries, was summoned to write the secret by the members of the Bishop's Commission. At that time, he was going through great difficulties. The little seminary of Visoko was getting ready to send him back because of scholastic deficiency. This great timid person wrote no matter what, in order to withdraw from the matter. The graphologists have observed that his writing reveals a profound anxiety, and he has maintained from this somber adventure, the confused reminder that he had not "written anything." In fact, he had written something. . .of insignificance. This rural trickery which he had improvised in his embarrassment, he regretted with bitter tears which had been compared to those of St. Peter. Overwhelmed from all sides, both private and public, this young man, then fragile, overcame the shock and overcame his feelings with peace and in humility.

17. The Secrets: The visionaries do not compare among themselves the secrets which they had received each by their count. They could then be different. The different compromises attest to the basic agreement, particularly evident for the third secret (the sign), and for the seventh, which has been "softened" according to Mirjana, but which has been "eliminated," according to others. There is then room for divergence of details, but not for 60 secrets!

18. It is true that Mirjana and Ivanka say that they received a piece of paper from the Gospa. But their two pieces of paper are of a different nature. On Mirjana's, the ten secrets are written in a yet invisible manner, which will manifest itself at the moment of revelation. As for Ivanka, she only received a code in order to write certain secret messages without risking their disclosure. I expressed several times my questions and reservations regarding these unusual particulars, which would make one think of magic. In the absence of having seen these pieces of paper keeping the secrets, one will have to wait their disclosure in order to judge them.

19. Again Ivan: (See note 16 above). Contrary to what the bishop says, Ivan well recognized that the Blessed Virgin reprimanded him and he was bitterly sorry for the error of his timidity which

was driven into entrenchment without a solution (*Latest News*). It is wrong to say: the Gospa, who did not authorize five visionaries to write the secret, contradicted herself by authorizing Ivan to do it. For if the five visionaries consulted the Gospa on this point, Ivan was caught off his guard and had to handle it by himself without having referred to it.

20. The hidden diary which Msgr. Zanic attributes to Vicka does not exist. She submitted to the Commission what she was able to submit (and from which I have given large excerpts). But the hidden diary which Msgr. Zanic attributes to her does not exist. Fr. Grafenauer has confirmed it. It was Fr. Grafenauer who collected and submitted to Msgr. Zanic the offending messages of Vicka on the different sheets of paper where he had noted this and that.

    Msgr. Zanic repeats here in a humble and edifying manner that he is ready to go on his knees from Mostar to Medjugorje if the sign of the visionaries manifests itself some day. For my part, I do not attach so much importance to this sign. The essential of Medjugorje is elsewhere.

21. Calumnies against the bishop? Jozo Zovko is a witness that Msgr. Zanic was favorable and enthusiastic about the apparitions. A cardinal who heard the bishop in Rome, during the summer of 1981, confirmed this to me. Msgr. Zanic seems to have forgotten his feelings from July-August, 1981. He affirmed then, while preaching confirmation in Medjugorje on July 25: "No, the visionaries are not lying; they are not lying. . ." He has forgotten it when he accuses them of lying six years later at the confirmation of July 25, 1987. But the recording of July 25, 1981, attests to his first favor.

22. There is an error of interpretation here: Jozo Zovko did speak of the danger of "wolves" and of "hypocrites," but he was aiming his terms enveloped in prudence, not at the bishop, but the Communist party who had arrested him and was subjecting him to a severe trial.

23. The calumny attributed to Tomislav Vlasic: Tomislav Vlasic spoke of the dangers which the devil puts Medjugorje through

but without identifying the bishop as the devil, as Msgr. Zanic pretends, through one of those subtle transfers of which he is a master.

24. The hidden truth. Msgr. Zanic, who repeats himself, takes up here the refuted accusation above (note 3). What he reproaches me to have hidden in the course of this memorandum, I have spoken of no matter how delicate certain topics may be. But he has only a very partial knowledge of my works. I understand that it may be difficult for him to read everything, and that he prefers to read the adversaries of Medjugorje. Still, he presumes my silence when he has not read my works.

25. According to his method which is polarized on evil (real or imagined), Msgr. Zanic closes his eyes to what is good; denies the cures which have brought about so many acts of thanksgiving and have impressed the doctors. He avoided every serious investigation on these cures, which he preferred to deny en masse. On the contrary, he has tried with scrupulous care to record those who have died after having come to Medjugorje, or after one had prayed for someone in Medjugorje. This method, which consists in burying the cures and exhuming the dead, is surprising.

26. Concerning the matter of Herzegovina (this conflict between the Bishop and the Franciscans which passion has not ceased to aggravate), is a foreign interference in the apparitions. Msgr. Zanic devotes himself to confusing these two events. The conflict between two priests in Mostar with the Bishop is foreign to Medjugorje. It is important to place this unfortunate interference for what it is: the tearful visit to Medjugorje of two priests who were being punished, the compassion of the visionaries, their indiscreet questions to the Blessed Virgin, and the imbroglio which resulted from it. We detailed it in *Messages and Teachings*.

27. Opinion of the Yugoslav Bishops. We leave Msgr. Zanic the responsibility of his evaluation. What is true is that in his presence, episcopal solidarity maintains silence in those who would be favorable to the apparitions, so it is difficult to identify them. On the contrary, those who have something to say in the mean-

ing of Msgr. Zanic, say it willingly. It is that which paralyzes the debates and continues to extend the expiration date, for a rapid investigation and decision had been foreseen. Everything was ripe in 1988. But they preferred to follow new studies (which could have as their interest) to gain time.

28. See *Apparitions Prolonged,* no. 5.

29. Let us also leave these two statements to the responsibility of Msgr. Zanic. We have shown some reservations on the evaluations of opinion in *Latest News,* Vol. 5 and 6.

30. Blindness and Fanaticism of Sects: According to his method, Msgr. Zanic continues to combine or to assimilate the apparitions of Medjugorje with the grossest errors suitable to discredit them. But there is not the least comparison to make between Medjugorje and these two deplorable matters which he evokes with complacency. Comparison is not reason.

    As far as the rosaries turning gold, see *Eight Years,* pp. 50-53.

31. It is true that numerous bishops have been pilgrims to Medjugorje. And some had consulted directly with the Pope before going there. Approximately 100 have come discreetly. But for the ninth anniversary, three of them wore their violet skull cap while presiding at a con-celebration: Msgr. Hnilica, the principal one, before approximately 50,000 people. On my trip in May 1990, a bishop from Ecuador con-celebrated with a purple skull cap. And I was near an Italian archbishop who had been opposed to Medjugorje for a long time, but his investigation made him favorable. It is not a matter then of a blindness, but, on the contrary, of a light acquired through methodical examination. The archbishop of whom I speak was opposed to Vicka's speaking in his cathedral, where some had invited her. When he arrived at her house on May 27, 1990, he said to her basically: "I had refused to welcome you in my house; are you going to refuse to welcome me in yours?"

    Vicka dismissed this contentious matter with a friendly gesture and a welcoming smile in her warm style.

32. One can only congratulate Msgr. Zanic for not publishing these offenses of which he speaks. To whose advantage? But he con-

tradicts what he repeats in no. 2: "He is not honest; he is guilty of hiding unpleasant things."

33. The boycott has been carried rather in another sense. No one has had more echoes and occasions to express himself in the media than Msgr. Zanic or Louis Belanger. I have met, for my part, more refusals to speak and publish.

PUBLISHER'S SPECIAL NOTE

The foregoing pamphlet of Bishop Zanic, after he was removed by Rome from any position of discernment regarding the apparitions and further asked to remain silent on the matter, caused numerous responses.

Such a response was written by Fr. Ljudevit Rupcic. Dr. Rupcic, a Yugoslav priest, received his doctorate in Sacred Scripture in 1958. He served on the Theological Commission of the Yugoslav Bishops' Conference from 1969 to 1980. He has also translated the New Testament into Croatian. He also was imprisoned twice by the Yugoslav Communist regime: in 1948, and again in 1956. He has written many books, and his latest is the response to Bishop Zanic titled, *The Truth About Medjugorje—A Response.*

The book was printed in Yugoslavia, as well as translated into English and the English edition was printed there also. It is a very candid, direct, forceful, and to some, shocking reply against the Bishop's allegations.

Since all the "created sensationalism" seems to come from the antagonists of Medjugorje, it is believed it is now time to reveal some of the heretofore un-published background regarding these attacks.

The book, *The Truth About Medjugorje*, can be obtained from the RIEHLE FOUNDATION, P.O. Box 7, Milford, OH 45150.

It should also be noted that in early January, 1991, a certain press release was distributed, worldwide, worded so as to imply a negative judgment regarding the events in Medjugorje. This release continues to be one of great controversy, confusion to Church authorities, and the basis for additional responses and clarifications. It will be covered in depth in the next book by Fr. Laurentin regarding Medjugorje, in the Fall, 1991.

Basically, this press release, formulated by Bishop Zanic, stemmed from a special meeting of the Bishops' Conference of Yugoslavia in Zagreb, November 27-28, 1990. It appears the result of this meeting had some connection with the visit of Bishop Komarica to Medjugorje on October 21, 1990, where he celebrated Mass and through his homily, called for the Yugoslav Bishops to visit the site and participate in the liturgies.

This apparent positive position, prompted the Bishops' Conference to issue a statement on Medjugorje at their November 27-28 session, at the prompting of Bishop Zanic. The statement, prepared only for the Vatican and not intended for release to the press, neither approved nor condemned the apparitions and left the matter undecided. The statement leaked to the press claimed otherwise.

In an effort to further clarify the situation, Bishop Djuro Koksa, of Zagreb, in an interview of January 9, 1991, stated:

"The bishops recognize that there are certain positive things at Medjugorje, for example, confessions, prayer and doing penance. The Bishops don't want to be deaf and dumb about this. Individual Catholics around the world should feel free to come to Medjugorje, but they should realize that Medjugorje is not like Lourdes, where Marian apparitions are declared credible."

Since this book by Fr. Laurentin was published in France in the Fall of 1990, the above sequences are not covered herein, but will be so in the subsequent issue. However, the publisher felt the need to add this special note for clarification. Further books by Fr. Laurentin, and the book by Fr. Rupcic, noted above, can be obtained by contacting The Riehle Foundation. A listing is shown on the last page of this book.

Number 3

THE END OF THE APPARITIONS
EXPECTED BY JULY 4, 1981

A Real Problem

Here Monsignor Zanic raised a real problem, but unfortunately, he distorts the information. It is true that on June 30, the visionaries expected the end of the apparitions by July 4.

But it is false that four or five times they attributed it to some "information from the Gospa." Only Mirjana and Ivanka referred to it (each one, only once) in the course of the confusing and fatiguing conversation recorded on a tape recorder at the presbytery on the evening of June 30, on return from the apparition at Cerno: "I asked her how many days she is going to stay with us. She answered, 'Three days,' " said Mirjana.

The other visionaries admitted it. That is perhaps the reason why Ivanka, asked where this idea came from, answered (according to Mirjana?): "From the Gospa."

At that time, all were thrust into some inextricable difficulties with the crowds, the police, fatigue. They felt completely overtaken by the events. The end of the apparitions was a solution within their capabilities.

What the Visionaries Said

The interrogation of that day showed some wavering. On the morning of June 30, Ivanka gave this response from the Gospa to the question: How many times will you appear?
—*As long as you wish, as long as you will want.*

As far as Mirjana was concerned, that morning she was persuaded that it would last only two or three days, but she did not attribute it to the Gospa: ("Something tells me—two or three more days.")

How did she plan a few hours afterwards, this premonition which dwelt in her concerning a response, undoubtedly ambiguous, from the Blessed Virgin? She does not remember about it.

In order to explain this error of the visionaries, some have made up an explanation which I have heard a hundred times: Since the visionaries received, during those days, a book of the 18 apparitions of Lourdes, they would have concluded from it that the Blessed Virgin would appear to them likewise, 18 times. But never, in many recorded dialogues, did the visionaries advance this explanation. And if they had thought 18 times, that would not lead at all to July 4, but to the 11th. Those who maintain this explanation explain it by saying: the Gospa appeared and disappeared several times in the course of the same apparitions. The visionaries then would have counted 15 apparitions from the date when they spoke (June 30), be it two or three apparitions each day during the first seven days. But then, how could they have been able to say "still three days?" On the morning after, there could have been two or three apparitions. The presumed calculation does not work in any sense or in any manner. In fact, the visionaries were little set on numbers and on chronology.

An Obscure Point

I questioned them systematically on this point. They cannot remember exact dates, and they are unable to clarify this point, which will always remain as an obscure part for history, as often happens. Msgr. Zanic, then, is right in posing this as a problem. We have understood the confusion of the visionaries. One thus understands that the problem is soluble. But we will not hold back the elements of a clear solution.

CURES: WHERE IS THE TRUTH?

In the previous article of Msgr. Zanic, he unilaterally cites the balanced warnings of Dr. Mangiapan, President of the Medical Bureau of Lourdes until Easter 1990. He maintains only the negative side:

"The allegations of cures are without merit, as a complete record has not been prepared and examined. This is the evidence itself."

But in other respects, Dr. Mangiapan recognizes the interest of the first submissions, while saying in particular: "The relatively important number of (alleged) cures can be placed on a parallel with what Dr. Saint-Maclou called (at the beginning of Lourdes) the miracle of numbers.

"Nine observations would merit a well researched investigation.
—The four cases of child illnesses,
—Four cases of tumors (specially one of them),
—Finally the case of kidney infection treated by dialysis.

"Nine cases of interest out of 58 alleged, is a very good number," I wrote to the author (Laurentin), and especially if they were confirmed based on a more indepth analysis."

It is not I then who hides the truth, integrally produced since 1984 in my first book. It is Msgr. Zanic who, according to his method, maintains and gives flavor to the negative and remains silent about the positive; that is what he calls a lie among his adversaries. Why falsify the judgment of Dr. Mangiapan by citing only two sentences drawn from the context, and falsified by an addition?

The study of the record has progressed.

a. The Italian doctors have kept for examination some twenty cases for which one can hope to establish a record. In Lourdes, after 122 years, one has been able to recognize only 58 miracles. In Medjugorje in less than 10 years, some 20 dossiers are on the right track. It is remarkable.

b. The medical subcommittee of the Yugoslav episcopacy has maintained two cures whose complete files match those of the best cures of Lourdes:

> 1) Diana Basile, cured instantaneously from multiple sclerosis, had experienced motor problems of four of her limbs, blindness of the right eye, and total urinary incontinence, with a skin irritation in this area. If Dr. Mangiapan expressed any reservations on the partial dossier which had been communicated to him, it is that the diagnosis of multiple sclerosis poses problems which cannot definitely be raised except through autopsy, thus after death.

Only three cures of multiple sclerosis were officially recognized in Lourdes by that remarkable specialist, Dr. Thiebaud. Diana Basile's case merits a more modern and more complete dossier than the cures of Lourdes. If one challenges it, it would also be necessary to challenge the three miracles recognized at Lourdes.

> 2) Damir Coric, cured from an internal hydrocephalus with important cerebral destructions verified by an tomography. This bed-ridden invalid is today in good health. He has returned to work again. We have more than once mentioned his case, notably in *Seven Years*. It is the case which Dr. Korljan considers the most remarkable.

Number 4

LETTER FROM THE PRIESTS OF THE PARISH OF MEDJUGORJE TO MSGR. ZANIC
(March 12, 1990)

Fr. Bishop,

We have received your short treatise entitled "Medjugorje." We regret that you have written and signed it, not because of the reputation of Medjugorje, but because of your reputation as a person, and even more as our bishop. This document resembles more a pamphlet than a letter from a bishop.

We regret that you, our bishop, see only blemishes in the events of Medjugorje. Medjugorje is in your diocese, less than 30 kilometers from your residence. In the last nine years Medjugorje has become a religious phenomenon of world influence. From year to year, this place is visited by tens of bishops, thousands of priests, and hundreds of thousands of pilgrims from the whole world. Most of them have a positive personal experience at Medjugorje. They do not consider themselves under illusion, won over, or deceived.

The Franciscans in Medjugorje have invited you repeatedly, in as much as you are bishop of the place, to come to Medjugorje and help improve their parish service, to hear confessions, preach, and observe their pastoral work. They desire to collaborate with you in everything as priests held responsible for collaborating with their bishop.

Through this letter then, in spite of everything that has taken place, we ask you to come more often to Medjugorje, to be with us, to share with us the burdens of the day, to observe the events up close, to also feed this portion of the flock which God gives you and entrusts to you.

Then, we are deeply convinced that you will not feel so grieved by such improvised statements from Vicka, or by Ivan's inexperience, but you will be personally able to experience the merciful love and the pardon of our God. Finally, you will be convinced that the faults of each priest have not succeeded in separating the people from Medjugorje. We dare to hope that it will not displease you, if you join our vision of the events of Medjugorje. (Letter to the Commission of the Yugoslav Episcopal Conference for Medjugorje, September 22, 1989; November 7, 1989; and February 21, 1990).

The collaborators of your Episcopal ministry:

P. Leonard Orec	P. Dobroslav Stojic
P. Victor Kosir	P. Ivan Landeka
P. Petar Ljubicic	

Number 5

COMMENTARY FROM *GLAS KONCILA*
Principal Croatian Periodical
(March 18, 1990)

We do not intend to express our judgment on the authenticity of the apparitions of which they speak in Medjugorje. The competent Commission will express it and someday probably also, the superior ecclesiastic authority. Even then, after the decision of this ecclesiastical authority, there is no obligation of conscience to believe or not to believe in the apparitions. It will oblige only the responsible officials of the Church either to permit, or not to permit, the worship of Our Lady under this title. In other words, the authority of the Church cannot oblige the faithful to believe what has not been contained in Revelation which is regarded as closed with the end of the apostolic era. It can only state that a new private revelation, or some devotions bound to these revelations, are not in contradiction to the whole of the Christian faith and can then be recognized.

With respect to the greatest or least holiness of the visionaries and of the different responsible people of the pastoral in Medjugorje, it is necessary to state that it does not constitute any proof either in favor or against the apparitions. It is known that different miracles, prophesies, visions, and manifestations of clear sightedness can be verified not only in holy persons but also among sinners, as several places, several passages in the Bible testify. In fact, it is a matter of divine gifts which are not merited, which by themselves do not grant sanctity and do not presuppose it. It goes from that, that this close proximity to the sacred realities should always stimulate the visionaries to a greater sanctity and from them—so too the priests and all those who are most involved in the Church—one expects them to live in sanctity as much as possible.

Therefore, whoever is going to dig into the private lives of the visionaries and of the other followers of the sanctuary, whoever does research and disseminates to the four winds their real or imagined weaknesses, in order to prove by it the falseness of the apparitions, obviously does not know the method and the practice of the Church and more specially, does not fear God Who defends not only calumny, but also defamation. To reveal the real or simply imagined sins of another, is a sin of defamation which can be very grave.

Number 6

"SLAIN IN THE SPIRIT"

Fr. Jozo Zovko (like Tomislav Vlasic) is a man of God, dangerous to Satan. They suffer his attacks. It is classical, including some calumnies and some measures intended to paralyze their activity. For Jozo Zovko it was arrest, then prison, then a surprising liberation, prohibition to preach in Medjugorje, etc.

These men of God, whatever their charity and humility may be, have something that surprises and at times troubles. They are vulnerable as always when God gives His servants some lead over human views. A new experience has surprised or shocked pilgrims going to Tihaljina. It happens that when Jozo Zovko imposes his hands on some pilgrims after a lengthy meditation, they fall on the floor (often referred to as "Slain in the Spirit"). Some lie on the ground, calm and silent, and get up a little later, calm, strong and normal. These falls surprise and upset some people.

"Illuminism, magical or psychological action, experiences that," someone said. "It is necessary to stop it."

One cannot speak of illuminism or exaltation; it is all the contrary: a kind of annihilation and renunciation of oneself before God. It is a special form of what has been called for a long time, "Slain in the Spirit." What is there to say? Many people are uptight, contracted, blocked, full of defenses before God, before men, and with respect to themselves, little disposed to enter into what is the mystical call, "the passive ways," a state of total receptivity to the discreet and the transcendent grace of God. "Rest in the Spirit" is a state of abandonment and total relaxation, in reception and in love. One can attain it in prayer without a fall or physical phenomenon, through the "prayer of peacefulness."

Then, who benefits from these falls? Should one combat this peculiarity?

Neither combat nor artificially provoke this phenomenon. The ways of God are not always those of men, these rational animals whom God invites to share in His eternal life, like the angels, or even above the angels like the Virgin Mary. But the rational animal, a sensitive being, goes to an invisible God through visible means, which mobilize his body and his organism. If these means are good and produce good fruits, why give them up?

Certainly, the essential visible means are the sacraments, but there are a lot of sacramentals and signs. To speak in tongues (which played an important role among the charismatics) and the gift of tears (frequent in Medjugorje among the sinners who go to confession) play a role similar to those who fall and find rest in the Spirit. The common point of these three gifts is a surpassing of stiffness, of rationalism, and of self-defense for an abandonment and complete relaxation: physical, psychic, spiritual before God, before oneself, and before mankind. It is an abandonment of our defenses and a complete relaxation.

For whom is it useful? It is difficult to discern *a priori*.

It was in Juarez that I best understood the function of this gift. The community of Rick Thomas (a community of poor people) felt called to visit the Mexican prisons where the unfortunate lived crowded in iron bar cages, in dark basements, like beasts, sickly and shriveled for lack of sun. In the psychiatric hospital, certain patients had to be protected from the dangers of their violent state with strait jackets or in padded cages. The prayer of Rick Thomas over these unfortunate ones often provoked, without anyone expecting it, the repose in the Spirit. The most prolonged prayer would plunge them into abandonment and peace. They would get up completely different, physically, psychologically, and spiritually freed.

One cannot react *a priori* and externally over the ways of God and the signs which He uses at the moment, on the scale of human frailty.

Let us be careful in condemning. Let us also be careful in artificially provoking these phenomena, or of cultivating them in a spectacular way as certain sects do. It is a grace to be taken as it comes, with discernment, modesty, and humility. Fr. Jozo is a man of discernment, and like all men of discernment, he knows how to develop and correct his options in view of the fruits and according to the light of God.

To widen the perspective, I would say the same thing of those luminous signs, those aromas, which some people perceive in Medjugorje. Having seen the complexity of these phenomena, I have not been able to sufficiently produce an adequate scientific study. I do not see proofs there, though some established prodigies. The proof will most always be impossible for the aromas. For millions of people, these unusual phenoma perceptions have been the sign which has opened their hearts (at times tightly closed) to the light of God and to the grace of conversion, which flourishes in Medjugorje. Let us not be scandalized so quickly when God humbly places Himself within the range of human frailty.

CHRONOLOGY

1989

February 9-11: Vicka's pilgrimage to Lourdes with an Italian group from Vicenza. Each day she had the apparition discreetly: on February 9 at the Agnus Dei of the Mass celebrated by Fr. Gianni Sgreva about 4 p.m.; on the 10th, at her hotel room with her sister, Anna; and on the 11th, at 3 p.m. while praying at the Grotto.

May 24: Through a letter addressed to the Provincial Curia of the Franciscans, Msgr. Zanic annuls the election of Jozo Zovko to the presbyterial council, and puts an end to his functions as parish priest of Medjugorje.

June 1: The editorial group of the Communist newspaper *Vjesnik,* from Zagreb, publishes a book entitled *Gospa in Medjugorje,* whose very positive tenor estimates the number of pilgrims at 11 million from 110 countries, including 20,000 American charters.

July 11: Msgr. Zanic calls Fr. Jozo Zovko to the bishopric, and reads to him two anonymous accusations against him. Fr. Jozo declares them slanderous and without basis. The bishop reproaches him for having made a second Medjugorje of his parish of Tihaljina.

July 14: On the night of July 13-14, a woman doctor from Bologna was cured from cancer. They should have operated on five vertebrae and she would have been paralyzed. Although belonging to an atheistic family, she was open to the workings of God. On July 13, the day before the operation, a friend came from Medjugorje and brought her a little bottle of blessed water. The following night, she experienced irresistible pain, found the little bottle, painfully opened it, and drank. Then there was a change and a feeling as though a hand passed over her back which cured it. She returned to bed and went to sleep. The next morning, she felt so well that she no longer wanted to be operated on. She was cured. The doctors analyzed the content of the little bottle: some simple water. She later came to Medjugorje on a pilgrimage of thanksgiving. "A drop of water in the hands of the Gospa is worth all the medicine. We can trust in the Madonna," concluded Fr. Jozo, who received her testimony.

July 18: Msgr. Zanic calls for a discussion against the purchase of land for the construction of buildings necessary for the immense center of pilgrimage.

July 20: Msgr. Zanic writes to the parish of Medjugorje to protest against the acquisitions and arrangements undertaken for the organization of the place of pilgrimage. He urgently gives the order that the apparitions not take place in any parish locale "because these are not apparitions and the Madonna is not at all present in this game."

July 24: Fr. John Vaughn, General of the Franciscans, informs Msgr. Zanic that the Franciscans of his diocese want to give the parishes of Jablanika and Nevesinje, reclaimed by him, to the secular clergy.

August 6-15: Closing of the "Year of the Youth," with participation by thousands of young people.

August 23: Msgr. Zanic deprives Fr. Jozo of his jurisdiction over the parish of Thijalina and names in his place, Fr. Zrinko Cuvalo, who was his vicar in Medjugorje in 1981. Fr. Jozo remains in the parish in agreement with the new priest. Msgr. Zanic deprives Fr. Leonard Orec, curé of Medjugorje for a year, of his jurisdiction over the parish at Medjugorje.

August 30: Fr. Jozo Zovko responds to the bishop, protesting against two anonymous calumnies which had been read to him on July 11 by Msgr. Zanic on the occasion of the inspection of his parochial accountability at the bishopric at Mostar. He respectfully requested the bishop to reexamine his decisions for the good of souls. He called on the numerous conversions, Christian marriages, and adult baptisms which have followed his instructions and conferences in Thijalina.

August: The priests of the parish of Medjugorje respond to the bishop, in order to justify the pastoral needs of Medjugorje, which compel them to some acquisitions and arrangements, notably the coming of thousands of priests and 50 bishops and cardinals for the year of 1989 alone and yet incomplete, without counting those who came incognito. They report the spiritual fruits of conversions, fasting, prayer, with a world record of confessions. They assure the bishop of their respect and their daily prayers and ask him respectfully for his help.

September 16: Marriage of Mirjana to Marco Soldo, celebrated in Medjugorje by Fr. Milan Mikulic, a Croatian Franciscan, stationed in the United States.

1990

January 30-February 14: Trip by Mirjana and her husband to Portland, Oregon.

Beginning of March: Msgr. Zanic sends to the Episcopal Conference, the Commission, and the world press, a new pamphlet against Medjugorje, *The Truth About Medjugorje* (16 pages), where he takes up again his objections and customary attacks.

March 10: Oberto (the drug addict reborn in Medjugorje: *Eight Years,* no. 8, pg. 147) was the victim of an accident near Munich. A car smashed into his old DS Citroen. This car, which had been given to him by the family, had been demolished, but he was unharmed. From March 20 to the beginning of April, he made a extended fast at the Center of Dr. Bauer (Arosa, Switzerland). During this time, the erroneous news of his supposed death arrived in Medjugorje, and his friends even celebrated his funeral Mass. His return to Medjugorje caused amazement throughout the area.

March 11, 1 p.m.: Death of Vicka's grandmother, aged 96, in the room where Vicka has the apparitions. It was this grandmother who had invited the visionaries to sprinkle holy water in order to prove the identity of the apparition.

March 12: The priests of the parish of Medjugorje protest against the pamphlet published by Msgr. Zanic. They ask him for his help and his participation in the services of this fruitful and worldwide place of pilgrimage. In the course of March, Msgr. Franic, retired archbishop of Split, writes to Msgr. Zanic, who had named him as one of the supporting columns of Medjugorje along with Rupcic, Faricy, Amorth, and some charismatic Franciscans from the whole world. He does it with a paternal calm, and mystic tone. Msgr. Zanic had been one of Msgr. Franic's priests; it was he who had Msgr. Zanic promoted to the episcopacy.

March 18: Mirjana, 25 years old, has her eighth anniversary apparition in her home in Medjugorje, near the place of the first apparition, from 7:15 to 7:21 in the evening. The Blessed Virgin speaks to her about the importance of the Mass and of the secrets. Her tears flow.

March 20-29: Medjugorje weekend at Duquesne University, Pittsburgh, Pennsylvania, with 5,900 registrants. They had to close the list for lack of space. Ivanka was present at this conference with her husband and little Kristina. She did not speak, but recited the Rosary. She stayed in the United States until the beginning of April.

March 25: Conference of ARPA (Catholic Medical Association for the Protection of Life and the Study of the Apparitions), in Rome with Vicka and Jakov who had come in two cars with Fr. Leonard Orec. 15,000 participants. Out of prudence, the Vatican preferred that the Pope not celebrate their Mass which filled St. Peter's Basilica in Rome. Nevertheless, he greeted the pilgrims from his window. Jakov did not have any apparitions in Rome; and Vicka had them discreetly, in private, in the morning.

April 7: Large Medjugorje conference in Banneux (Belgium), with Vicka's participation.

April 8: Second meeting at Beauraing with Vicka.

April 22: Election in Croatia, first round.

April 24-26: Meeting of the Episcopal Conference in Zagreb. Medjugorje is on the program. But in the current conditions, any decisions were postponed. "The Commission continues its work," they concluded.

May 4: Giovanna Spanu, from Sardinia, who had multiple sclerosis, disabled since 1970, was recommended to Vicka's prayers. She felt capable of climbing the hill of the apparitions with the help of her friends, and there she experienced a warmth which spread over her entire body. She was able to stand alone and came down the hill without any assistance. She had found again her equilibrium which had been totally lost; her normal motor functions, and the terrible crises which she suffered had ended. On the next day, at noon, she came to declare her cure at the presbytery.

May 6: Election in Croatia, second round. Cardinal Kuharic, Archbishop of Zagreb and president of the Episcopal Conference, and the Islamic and Jewish religious authorities were invited into the hemi-cycle of the assembly. The Orthodox metropolitan, likewise invited, did not come. The Croatians danced with joy before this new birth of the free Croatia after centuries. Dr. Korljan, in charge of the Medical and Scientific Sub-committee of Medjugorje, whose conclusions are totally favorable to the apparitions, was president of one of the parties founded in haste. He had not wanted to be present at the elections, but his daughter was elected in Zagreb. Cardinal Kuharic responds this same day (prudently) to questions of the Italian television (I saw the tape).

May 13-15: Conference on Medjugorje at Notre Dame (Indiana, USA): 6,000 people. Msgr. Franic, Archbishop Emeritus of Split, invited to this conference, reveals in the course of an interview: "I have heard three times, inside of me, the voice of Our Lady.

I had not entrusted this to anyone until now. It was a personal message which ended in convincing me. It is deeply engraved in my memory."

May 27-31: My twenty-second trip to Medjugorje.

June 9: Msgr. Zanic gives the Sacrament of Confirmation to the parish of Medjugorje. Fr. Leonard Orec had established contacts with his secretary, who had assured him that the bishop would speak only of confirmation and not against Medjugorje, as he did the preceding time (July 25, 1987). Fr. Orec asked the pilgrims to stay away from the church during the ceremony, and to leave it for the parishioners alone, in order to avoid any interference.

June 9 (Following): Msgr. Zanic worthily celebrated the Sacrament. In brief, this time it was a cordial understanding to the contentment of all, including the bishop.

June 14: Birth of Josyp Elez, Ivanka's second child.

June 25: Ninth anniversary concelebrated by Msgr. Hnilica, preached by Fr. Kustic, before 50,000 people. A little before 7 o'clock, fifth annual apparition to Ivanka in her home, without witnesses except her family, her father, her grandmother, and two Irish guests. The apparition lasted nine minutes. Ivanka saw her mother again for one minute. The Blessed Virgin spoke to her about the fifth secret.

July 6-8: Medjugorje Conference at the University of Steubenville.

July 30-August 3: New International Week of Prayer (especially English-speaking) for young people in Medjugorje in the extension of the *"Year of the Youth,"* 1989. This week was followed by other weeks for other language groups: August 7-14 for Slovenes, Czechs, Polish; August 16-24 for the German speaking; August 20-September 1 for the Latin languages.

August 11-12: Medjugorje Peace Conference in Irvine, California (USA).

December 8-9: Conference on Medjugorje in New Orleans, USA.

1991

January: A new unauthorized press release, guided by Bishop Zanic, alledges "nothing supernatural at Medjugorje. (To be covered in depth in our subsequent book.)

MEDJUGORJE

The following books of Father Laurentin have been translated into English, and are currently available from The Riehle Foundation.

The Apparitions at Medjugorje Prolonged ($5)
By Fr. René Laurentin

Update book through June 1986.
Fifth anniversary, news of the seers, scientific studies, the messages.

Latest News of Medjugorje ($4)
By Fr. René Laurentin

Update book through June 1987.
The marriage of Ivanka, response to the objections, information on the new commission.

Seven Years of Apparitions ($5)
By Fr. René Laurentin

Update book current through Fall 1988.
Sixth anniversary, the controversies, testimonies, the fruits.

Eight Years ($5)
By Fr. René Laurentin

Update book through July 1989.
Seventh and eighth anniversaries, investigations, latest messages, wonderful interviews with the visionaries.

Messages and Teachings of Mary at Medjugorje ($7)
By Fr. René Laurentin

The chronological listing of over 700 messages from Medjugorje, applicable to Scripture and Catholic doctrine. Emphasis on the urgency for the world to return to God.

The Truth About Medjugorje—A Response ($5)
By Fr. Ljudevit Rupcic

Published in 1990. Dr. Rupcic's response to the pamphlet "Medjugorje" by Msgr. Zanic.

If you wish to receive copies, please write to:

THE RIEHLE FOUNDATION
P.O. Box 7
Milford, OH 45150

All contributions are used for the publishing and/or distribution costs of providing spiritual material to a world desperately in need of learning more about and living in God's peace and love.

THE
RIEHLE
FOUNDATION...

The Riehle Foundation is a non-profit, tax-exempt, charitable organization that exists to produce and/or distribute Catholic material to anyone, anywhere.

The Foundation is dedicated to the Mother of God and her role in the salvation of mankind. We believe that this role has not diminished in our time, but, on the contrary has become all the more apparent in this the era of Mary as recognized by Pope John Paul II, whom we strongly support.

During the past four years the foundation has distributed over two million books, films, rosaries, bibles, etc. to individuals, parishes, and organizations all over the world. Additionally, the foundation sends materials to missions and parishes in a dozen foreign countries.

Donations forwarded to The Riehle Foundation for the materials distributed provide our sole support. We appreciate your assistance, and request your prayers.

IN THE SERVICE OF JESUS AND MARY
All for the honor and glory of God!

The Riehle Foundation
P.O. Box 7
Milford, OH 45150